THE ASBURY REVIVAL

When God Used Students to Wake a Nation

WAYNE ATCHESON

SONCOAST
PUBLISHING

The Asbury Revival

Copyright © 2020 by Wayne Atcheson

First printing December, 2020

All rights reserved

ISBN 978-1-953406-05-7 Paperback

Cover Design by Abigail Jackson

Book design by Martine Fairbanks

Published by Soncoast Publishing

P.O. Box 1503

Hartselle, AL 35640

Printed in the United States of America

"It was as if the campus had been suddenly invaded by another Power. Classes were forgotten. Academic work came to a standstill. In a way awesome to behold, God had taken over the campus."

Dr. Robert E. Coleman

CONTENTS

Preface	vii
1. Author's First Visit To Asbury	1
2. How It Began – Two And A Half Years Before The Revival	7
3. Class Is Cancelled	13
4. President Dennis Kinlaw's Story	17
5. Tuesday Evening 11 P.M. – 13 Hours Have Passed	21
6. Thursday Morning – 48 Hours Have Passed	25
7. Friday 10:30 P.M. – 84 Hours Have Passed	31
8. Saturday Morning – 96 Hours Have Passed	35
9. Sunday Morning – 120 Hours Have Passed	37
10. Tears Continue To Flow Into Post Revival	41
11. The Tim Philpot Story – One Student's Amazing Account	43
12. A Bible Professor's Confession in Chapel	47
13. Revival Spread Across America – "The Less Impressive the Student Was, the More Effective an Instrument He Was"	49
14. Revival Reflections From President Kinlaw	53
15. For Months, Students Share, and Revival Breaks Out in Schools Across America	57
16. Revival Fire Spreads Powerfully And Miraculously	61
17. David Perry Goes on a Nine-Month Revival Crusade	69
18. David Perry's Revival Journey Begins With His Own Confession	73
19. Unknown Asbury Called "Hash-Bury"…"Has-Bury"…"Ash-Bury"	77
20. The Asbury Revival Flame Has Never Gone Out	83
21. 50 Years Later: February 2-3, 2020 Sunday Afternoon Hughes Auditorium	87
22. Beth Kinlaw Coppedge Imparts Moving Revival Moments	91

23. Steve Seamands Speaks of What He Saw and Heard	95
24. Former President Sandra Gray and President Kevin Brown Close Out the Afternoon Session	99
25. The 50th Anniversary Chapel Service in Hughes Auditorium	103
26. Stan Key Paints a Powerful Picture of Revival	107
27. Jeannine Brabon Message 50 Years Later	111
28. Jeannine....When Jesus Walked In And Revival Came	115
29. Tim Philpot Skips Chapel But Finds the Revival	121
30. The 50th Revival Reunion Ended With an Altar Call, Testimonies, and a Hymn Sing of Praise	127
31. Call to Revival	135
About the Author	143

PREFACE

As a boy growing up in Maplesville, Alabama in the 1940's, my daddy was a street preacher, tent revivalist, radio preacher and small-town country pastor/evangelist for 63 years. Maplesville is in the very heart of Alabama and had a population of 1,000 people. Most worked at the two veneer mills in town. It never had a stop light.

On summer Saturdays, people in the rural areas would come to town and buy their groceries; get their corn ground at the Grist Mill; get their gasoline at the three filling stations; enjoy seeing family, friends and strangers; treat themselves to an ice cream cone or a Coca Cola or RC Cola and Moon Pie; and stay most of the day. There were ten grocery stores and my grandfather and an uncle ran two side by side downtown. They all prospered well.

My Daddy had a passion to preach the Gospel. On many Saturdays in the summer months, he would place two loud speakers, as we called them, on the top of a 1939 Chevrolet, and my brother Gerald and I would go with him preaching on the streets of Brent, Centreville and Maplesville on Saturday morning, and Clanton, Thorsby and Jemison on Saturday afternoon. He would drive down the streets of those small towns, speak into a small handheld microphone behind the wheel, and announce over the speakers that he would be preaching at the end of the street in 10 or 15 minutes.

People would gather around and Daddy would play a Gospel song before he would preach for 15 minutes. His message was always to repent of your sins, make sure your salvation was secure in Jesus Christ, be involved in a church, and give your life to Christ and escape hell. It was always a Gospel message about the love of God, that He was not willing that any should perish, but that all may receive salvation for their souls. He preached boldly, passionately and with great authority.

So, I was raised on evangelism and revival. He also wore out three tents and at the age of eight, I walked the sawdust trail in his tent meeting at Billingsley Junction and knelt at an altar Daddy had built. The entire experience was exciting to me as a boy to see my father preaching on the street, in tent meetings, on the radio that lasted 53 years, and be pastor of 17 churches, mostly in rural areas. He had me singing on radio at age five. Daddy spent most of his years as a bi-vocational pastor. When he passed away in 2001 at age 89, he had preached his last sermon two months prior on his radio program. He was very frail and weak but he got through it.

My zeal for evangelism and revival was ingrained in my heart early on and is more alive in me today than ever before. In 2009, I began to teach Revival History and am certainly a student of it. I include the Wales Revival along with Revival in America that started with the First Awakening with Jonathan Edwards and George Whitefield, and the Second Awakening with Charles Finney.

As I studied Revival History, I became fascinated with the Asbury College student-led revivals. Asbury began in 1890 as a Wesleyan Methodist Holiness College, founded by John Wesley Hughes in Wilmore, Kentucky, a small town 18 miles south of Lexington. It was the first holiness college in America. I learned that Asbury had experienced 15 student led revivals on campus from 1907 until

2006. Asbury College became Asbury University in 2010, and today it is a private Christian, nondenominational liberal arts school.

Out of the 1907 revival came E. Stanley Jones, a student at Asbury who became a great missionary to India. Mighty movements of God took place over the years, but in 1970, perhaps the greatest broke out in chapel in Hughes Auditorium on February 3. The revival extended for a week and had a far reaching impact across America and beyond. Of all college revivals that I have studied and known about, this may have been the greatest student-led campus revival in American history. None were more impactful.

As I studied the Asbury revivals, I discovered a 37-minute DVD on the internet by Dr. Dennis Kinlaw, who was President of Asbury College at the time of the 1970 revival. Years after the revival, he was recorded at a gathering while telling the Asbury revival story. It affected me so that I have watched it dozens of times and am moved every time I see it. Of course, I have shown it many times to groups and shared it extensively.

Chapter One
AUTHOR'S FIRST VISIT TO ASBURY

In August of 2018, my wife Barbara and I went to Kentucky to see Noah's Ark, the Creation Museum and the site of the great Cain Ridge Revival that took place in 1801-1802 near Paris, which is 18 miles northeast of Lexington. What a blessing to take in this revival history known as the largest and most famous camp meeting of the Second Great Awakening!

After that special blessing, the next destination was one that I had longed to visit, Asbury College in Wilmore, Kentucky. Barbara's grandfather, Dr. Everett Freeman, was a 1915 graduate of Asbury and had a wonderful ministry in Kansas as a Methodist minister. His 1915 Asbury yearbook was handed down to Barbara, a leather bound book with 225 pages. It is a treasure. It means so much to have an Asbury graduate in our family. He lived to be 94 and died in 1984. He was a true disciple of Jesus Christ and he dearly loved the Methodist church. With great anticipation, we drove the 18 miles south of Lexington to Wilmore, and then Highway 29 led us right to the campus.

Barbara Atcheson pointing to her grandfather's picture

As we drove onto the circular drive of buildings, I looked for Hughes Auditorium. I spotted this stately red brick structure with huge white columns, and it took my breath away just to see it for the first time. We parked in front of it. It was a holy moment for me. I knew that it was a place where the Glory of the Lord Jesus had visited many times. It was like a "Holy of Holies" place to me, and the Spirit of the Lord began to rise within my heart and soul as we got out of our car to meet Mark Troyer, who was there to give us a tour of the campus. Mark is an Asbury vice-president and I had given him a tour of the Billy Graham Library a few months earlier.

We expressed our grateful appreciation for his time, and he was so gracious. However, my thoughts were on the great movements of God that had occurred in this holy place, Hughes Auditorium. As I approached the long steps out front, I found myself walking slowly as I knew I was about to enter a place where the Spirit of the Holy God had come in a most unusual way. It was a joyful feeling to be there, but on the other hand, I was slightly hesitant about walking in. I had never experienced such a feeling entering such a holy room.

We were talking but when I got to the lobby, I slowed up and stopped. For me, it was almost too sacred a place to walk into and the auditorium was completely empty. I knew that Jesus had come to this place and had never left. I sensed His power and presence as I slowly walked in, and my mind was racing in thought of all the things I had read and seen on film that had taken place in this large room of 1,500 old-fashion wooden theater-type seats. I was in awe and overwhelmed by the Spirit.

The three of us stood in the back as Mark spoke about its history. The lights were off but it was early in the afternoon, and as I looked toward the front, I saw a figure of a person walking up the aisle toward us. As this person got closer, I was startled to discover that it was Dr. Sandra Gray, the Asbury president, who came over to greet us. I had met Dr. Gray twice and expressed my great desire to visit Asbury someday and see the place of these great revivals. She seemed so pleased that we came, and the feeling was mutual.

When she walked up the aisle to greet us, I was taken with great surprise and for me, it was as if she represented all the great leaders of this godly college that had come out to welcome us. What a special welcome to Asbury! We felt so honored. Indeed, it was a glorious moment as we visited for a few moments, and she left to go back to her office.

Then the three of us made our way down to the large curved wooden altar where mighty Asbury student-led revivals had seen thousands kneel repenting and confessing their sins; getting right with God; receiving Jesus as Lord; receiving the baptism of the Holy Spirit; seeing sins forgiven; and for many, making commitments to give their lives as foreign missionaries and serving the Lord in full time surrender to Christian service. No doubt, buckets of tears had also fallen at this altar over the years. Barbara and I knelt and thanked God for great movements of God that had taken place here; praying that He would send another, and thanking him for the privilege of being there.

Since the Hughes Auditorium had been built in 1929, which makes it 91 years old, the words "HOLINESS UNTO THE LORD" were emblazoned above the organ pipes above the platform. How truly appropriate. Those words have rung true in this godly edifice over the decades. The 1915 Asburian yearbook said Asbury College was the first Holiness College in America.

We toured the campus for a couple of hours and even stayed overnight at the Asbury Inn and Suites on the seminary campus. Mark and Dr. Gray insisted that we come next year for their Hymn Sing at the Alumni Reunion. I marveled at the thought of attending a service in Hughes Auditorium. What a privilege that would be. God willing for me, I would be there. So, on June 21, 2019, I drove with great anticipation to Wilmore and was so excited about the Hymn Sing in a 91-year-old building known also for its acoustics and glorious singing.

I only knew two people out of 1,200 alums gathered on that Friday evening. Many came as foreign missionaries and others from across the nation. I discovered that the large name tags also gave the year of the class from which they graduated. So, I began to look for those who would have been students during the 1970 Revival. They would be from ages 68-71 now.

There was the usual hugging and greetings of classmates that you see at reunions. There was so much laughter, smiles and back slapping as they greeted one another. I took an aisle seat on the back row as Dr. Mark Schell, Professor of Church Music and Organ, began the long anticipated Hymn Sing. The 1,200 people present filled up the auditorium floor seating. To my delight, the first song announced was *And Can It Be*. I thought how appropriate, Billy Graham's favorite hymn. The only accompaniment was a piano and organ, just like the Graham crusades. The people sang with such passion.

Then Dr. Schell said, "Tonight we are going to sing 10 hymns." Each hymn was a particular class hymn. Those attending from that class would be asked to stand on the first verse, to their great delight. Dr Schell did a masterful job of telling hymn stories, mixing the male and female voices, and giving every alum joyful memories of Asbury chapel days. And yes, the mighty presence of the Lord Jesus filled the room.

As the songs were called out, I jotted them down in this order: 1. *O For A Thousand Tongues to Sing*; 2. *Victory in Jesus*; 3. *A Mighty Fortress Is*

Our God; 4. *All Hail The Power of Jesus Name*; 5. *Blessed Assurance*; 6. *The Solid Rock*; 7. *Be Thou My Vision*; 8. *Jesus Paid It All*; 9. *How Great Thou Art*; 10. *Wonderful Grace of Jesus*. They sang every verse of every song. To listen to these hymns sung by men and women who were fully surrendered to Jesus, many of whom had served or were serving in life-threatening areas abroad, sounded different than perhaps any other time in my life. It was praise to the Lord in holy songs of joy. There was a sweetness of the Holy Spirit. It was like Heaven came down and Glory filled their souls and mine. Their voices rang with purpose and meaning and every word meant something. They truly believed what they were singing.

Then this worship of praise and adoration to Almighty God seemed to end in their traditional way with their voices lifted to "*Praise God From Whom All Blessings Flow.*"

After the service, God had another special blessing waiting for me. I stood, observed names tags and mingled down the aisle toward the center. I spotted a couple, Bob and Sydney Biddulph, who were indeed students at Asbury in 1970. I introduced myself and they were delighted to talk about the revival they experienced as students. I told them I was going to write an account of the revival, and talk to as many alums as I could about what they remembered and the impact it had. Bob said, "You need to talk to Jeannine Brabon."

With a thousand people there and only knowing two people, I thought maybe I could get her phone number and call her later. As I was talking to Bob and Sydney, who were missionaries in Spain, a woman walked up beside me. I finished my short conversation with the couple and looked to see the woman's name tag. To my unbelief, the name tag read, "Jeannine Brabon." She was a dear friend of the couple and the prayer leader for the 1970 Revival. I knew then that God had a reason for me being at Asbury. To meet Jeannine so soon was amazing affirmation. Jeannine and I talked for several minutes, and we have been in touch frequently since she returned to the mission field in Colombia, South America, where she has served as a missionary since graduating from Asbury in 1971. She has been a tremendous help as I wrote this account of the Asbury College 1970 Revival Revisited.

It was a special privilege to visit with other 1970 students over the next two days, and to roam the campus, enjoy other services in Hughes Auditorium and learn more about its history and vision for years to come.

This 1970 Asbury revival account includes conversations with many students that I met during three visits to the Asbury campus in the past two years. Much of what I have accumulated has come with special permission from these sources. They include Dr. Robert Kanary, who wrote *Spontaneous Revivals, Asbury College 1905-2006, Firsthand Accounts of Lives Transformed*, which was published in 2017. Dr. Robert E. Coleman and Dr. David J. Gyertson edited *One Divine Moment* in 1970, and Rev. David T. Perry wrote, *The Asbury Revival of 1970*. It has been a joy to get acquainted with Dr. Kanary, Dr. Coleman, Dr. Gyertson and Rev. Perry in this exciting journey. Their encouragement has been such a blessing to me and spurred me on. Also, strong messages and resources about the Revival came from two videos, *The Asbury Revival 1970* with Dr. Dennis Kinlaw and *When God Comes*, a documentary by Broadman and Holman Publishers in 1995.

A book project requires much assistance and support. I'm so grateful to Raquel Arbogast, Emily Adams and Tim Siebert at the Billy Graham Evangelistic Association for their technology and editing support. Jennifer Sharpe for her superb editing expertise. My revival prayer team at BGEA who have followed this project from the beginning which includes Tom and Ouida Phillips, Bruce Snell and Emily Adams. And my loyal and supporting wife, Barbara, and daughters Elizabeth Poplin and Amy Snyder who have always cheered me on with the books I have written.

I have relied on Jeannine Brabon for total accuracy. What an honor to communicate regularly and get to know Jeannine, the revival prayer leader, in this project. She is a living revival giant.

Chapter Two

HOW IT BEGAN – TWO AND A HALF YEARS BEFORE THE REVIVAL

The key leader for the 1970 Asbury Revival was a missionary's daughter from Colombia, South America named Jeannine Brabon. She received a call herself to be a missionary at age 11. She said, "My hunger for God led me to surrender all and to let the Holy Spirit fill me. I entered into an intimate walk with Jesus and several years later, I was enrolled in a regimented boarding school in Florida, where many teenagers of missionaries attended. It was Hampden DuBose Academy in Zellwood, Florida. The Holy Spirit impressed me to pray every hour, and so I made 3x5 cards for every hour of the day, a set for each day of the week. It took me two months to organize but it became a lifelong habit.

"When I arrived as a freshman in 1967 at Asbury, God just put it on my heart to pray for revival on this campus. I sensed a spiritual drought here. I was aware of past student led revivals here, but this was a time when students on campuses across America were in rebellion over the Vietnam War and other unrest. Sin had creeped back onto campus in many ways, and there was a need for students to resist temptations and get their lives back in touch with God as committed Asbury students.

"So as a freshman, I started praying for students, faculty and administration. I would pray at all hours of the day. Quietly, I began interceding, passionate for God to come. God would remind me, 'Jeannine, your role on campus is to intercede.' I never told someone that I would pray for them without doing so. Active in sports, as I ran my mile, I would intercede. My freshman year, I never missed chapel, always expecting Jesus to come. I had never heard of the great revivals and awakenings of the past. However, I read the Scriptures and knew how desperately needy we were. I did not feel like I was anyone special on campus. I was a nobody. But to Jesus, I knew His heart for me, and I longed to pour myself out for all of God in my life.

"Chapel was required three days each week, Tuesday, Thursday and Saturday at that time. In spite of this requirement, many students were drifting away from God. Students were neglecting rules like curfew and hair length. There was even drug abuse. Asbury needed a touch from God.

"At the beginning of my junior year, I went to the Registrar's office and got a list of the entire student body. I put the list of every student in a three-ring binder. I carried this everywhere I went, as well as the prayer cards, on which I had already written many students names down, previously. Even in the cafeteria line, I would pull those cards out and pray for students, that God would work in their heart and life. It was something I did at various times of each day, never an idle moment. I had come to understand and live 'pray without ceasing.' God had set a fire in me for revival.

"Hour by hour, my soul was drawn out in prayer. At times, it seemed like a life and death struggle. At other times, it was like a confrontation with the fury of hell. Not an hour passed but what I felt the Spirit interceding. Even in my sleep, I found my soul crying out to God. Even though I was in college studying to get an education, the highest priority in my life was to know God and make Him known. I knew we needed God to step into our midst in a supernatural way. Only an outpouring of the Holy Spirit would make this possible." Even though Jeannine was shy and not very outgoing, her junior class elected her Class Chaplain.

In 1968, Jeannine posted a sign, "Come Apart To Pray" on a classroom door. A few students began to pray a half hour before each chapel. At a weekly fast prayer meeting in 1969, Jeannine and another student felt the need to pray all night. After getting permission from a Dean, an all-night service occurred in Hughes Auditorium on October 3 with 150 students in earnest prayer.

"That evening, I turned on the skylights in Hughes Auditorium about twenty minutes to midnight," says Jeannine. "A glow filled the place. The newly gold carpeted floor added warmth. Already, I felt God present. 'God,' I prayed, 'please come, show me I have seen nothing yet about the power of prayer.' How could I ever explain the passion for Jesus which burned in my heart? Shortly after 12 midnight, 10 men students entered and went directly to their knees at the altar. Within twenty minutes, 150 students poured into Hughes Auditorium.

"My heart soared with joy. We began praying all over the auditorium as one voice, the coming of the Holy Spirit, and the need for repentance. As a very needy people, we hungered for more of God. Scripture read covered the plan of salvation and included II Chronicles 7:14. Genuine heartfelt prayers of confessing of sin arose unabated. 'God forgive me.' Total freedom in the Holy Spirit to be transparent. Songs of redemption and praise acapella filled the air. I had never witnessed anything like this in my life.

"I went up to the back balcony in utter awe of the presence of God in our midst. The only professor present, Dr. Clarence Hunter, found me and asked, 'Jeannine, I am trying to find out who is in charge here.' No one was ever on the platform. 'Sir,' I responded, 'I believe it is the Holy Spirit.' Stroking his chin, he said, 'Don't you think God has met us? Why don't we go and thank Him?'

"So the 80 students, still present at 3 a.m. in the morning, gathered down front forming a circle around the altar and up around the pulpit on the platform. With our hands joined, we praised God that

He had answered our prayer and He would come in revival power. At nearly 4 a.m., I fell asleep, only to be up again in time for Saturday's 8 a.m. chapel in the same room.

"A student stopped me after chapel disappointed. She said, 'Jeannine, nothing happened today!' I said, 'Do you know what Acts 1:7 says?' 'It is not for you to know the times or seasons that the Father has placed in His hands. But, you shall receive power when the Holy Spirit comes.' God has answered our heart cry, and in His time, Jesus will come with revival power. We need to keep trusting, praising Him with pure hearts."

Jeannine Brabon's Yearbook Photo

This visitation of the Holy Spirit was a mere foretaste of what was to come exactly four months later on February 3. From that night of prayer came students who joined Jeannine and committed to pray for a movement of God on campus. In November, Jeannine adapted the John Wesley Great Experiment, a set of disciplines to go deeper with God. It began with six students and in January, 30 students were committed to Scripture reading, prayer, fasting and other disciplines.

On Saturday, January 31, students who did the John Wesley Great Experiment, shared their experiences in chapel. New President Dr. Dennis Kinlaw said, "It may have been the most impressive chapel service I had ever witnessed. They were inspiring the other students for a deeper walk with God."

THE DAY THE DIVINE MOMENT CAME

God's "Divine Moment" arrived three days later on Tuesday, February 3, 1970, as snow covered the ground and a cold wind whipped through the tall, barren trees on campus. Academic Dean Custer Reynolds was to speak at the 10 a.m. chapel, but was not impressed to speak but decided to give his testimony and open the floor to students who wished to share.

HOW IT BEGAN – TWO AND A HALF YEARS BEFORE THE REVIVAL • 11

As Jeannine took her seat in the Junior class section of the auditorium, she whispered to her chapel partner, Barb Bunn, "I have a test next hour." Her friend responded, "So do I, but I don't think we'll take them."

Hughes Auditorium

Jeannine remembers well what happened when chapel started. "A sigh of relief surged from the students when Dean Reynolds announced that he was only giving a short personal witness. Then, he said, 'I feel led to open this time for testimonies.' Almost immediately, across the middle section of Sophomore's and over to the Senior section, Larry Sutherland stood up and loudly spoke out, 'I want to confess. I've been a hypocrite, but recently God got a hold of me and I'm a new person. I love Jesus and have turned my life over to him. It's real. I am a different person.' Larry was known as the Gym Jamboree clown on campus. He was an all-around good athlete and one of the most popular students. He was supposed to have graduated the year before but didn't finish. His witness really got the students attention."

Dr. Howard Hanke, a professor of Bible, also recalls the shock of the assembly when Larry stood at his seat. He remembers Larry saying, "I'm not believing that I'm standing here telling you what God has done for me. I've wasted my time in college up to now, but Christ has met me, and I'm different. Last night the Holy Spirit flooded in and filled my life. Now, for the first time ever, I am excited about being a Christian! I wouldn't want to go back to the emptiness of yesterday for anything." Then Dr. Hanke added, "Others followed. Everyone sensed that something unusual was happening. God seemed very near.

"After Larry had shared his new found life in Christ, the Dean invited others to do the same. Quickly, a number of students stood to speak in various areas of the sanctuary. Their testimonies were fervent and reflected deep heart searching. Clichés were totally absent. Each person seemed intent upon sharing an up-to date report on what God was doing in his or her life.

"Sensing the mandate of the moment, one of the professors near the close of the allotted chapel hour, slipped to the platform and expressed that any student who wanted to pray should feel free to come to the altar. There was no pleading or cajoling – just the quiet reminder that the altar was open."

Chapter Three
CLASS IS CANCELLED

Jeannine also remembers the crucial transition moment in this way. "Now at this point, Dean Reynolds had to make a decision. Eddie Bonniwell nudged me and said, 'Jeannine, this cannot stop. God is here.' I said, 'Yes, He is. You go, Eddie, and tell the Dean.' He arrived upon the platform at the same time as Dr. Hunter. Both had the same message. Chapel must go on! Let God continue what He has begun. God in his providence had the Academic Dean to be in charge of chapel that day, as only he had the authority to do so. Then Dean Reynolds announced, 'Class is cancelled.' God had come down to Hughes Auditorium, and this visitation of His presence would continue in a powerful way 24-hours-a-day for the next seven days. We didn't have class for a week."

∽

Debbie Meyer

"I was one of those who entered chapel February 3, with the attitude of 'Oh no, another dull testimony service.' Later I was confronted with the reality that

> *the Spirit of God was in our midst and that He seemed to have no intention of leaving for quite some time. He had touched several of my friends and given them joy that came from their hearts and covered their faces. Finally, I realized that I was not claiming it as my own. After a time at the altar, where I gave everything to Jesus, I found the love and joy I had seen in others. Then I prayed my heart out for some of my friends that they would give Jesus everything and go away with nothing but His wonderful love, joy and peace."*

～

When the quiet reminder came that the altar was open, Dr. Hanke remembers that "No sooner had the invitation been extended than a mass of students moved forward. The congregation began singing *"Just As I Am."* There was not room for all who wanted to pray at the altar. Many had to kneel in the front seats of the auditorium. Their prayers were mingled with heartfelt contrition and outbursts of joy. It was evident that God was moving upon His people in power. The presence of the Lord was so real that all other interests seemed unimportant. The bell sounded for classes to begin, but it went unheeded.

"As scores of students flocked forward to pray, these young people made their way to the edge of the platform, hoping yet to be able to give their testimony. Those who had come to the altar, after a time of prayer, rose, joining those on the platform and with tears, made confessions. These acknowledgements ranged from cheating and theft, to having animosity, prejudice and jealousy.

"Some made their way to individuals in the congregation to ask forgiveness and to make restitution. Old enemies were melted with the fervent love of God. Frequently, these encounters of reconciliation resulted in experiences of joy and gladness. Some shook hands while others embraced. Often having obtained a new relationship with God, students would raise their fingers in the peace symbol---a V for victory sign. Students in all classes, freshmen to seniors, poured out their souls, asking for forgiveness and exhorting others to heed the call of God."

LUNCH TIME CAME AND NO ONE MOVED

Lincoln Stevens, a student, said, "Testimonies and confession continued through another hour, and then two. Then it was lunch time but still no one moved. I went to the dining hall and only a handful of people were there."

In the opening hours, members of the Women's Glee Club stood in their places around the auditorium and sang with fervor, "*When I Survey The Wondrous Cross*." Says Dr. Hanke, "One student, Jeff Blake, felt led to capture this 'Divine Moment' with written word and reflection. 'God came during those days. The God of the universe made his way to a remote spot on earth and I, one of His 3 billion children on this planet, found myself in the midst of one of His great divine moments in this century.' Out of a burning heart, Jeff began to acknowledge Acts 4:20 ... 'For we cannot but speak the things which we have seen and heard.'"

He wrote, "I sit in the middle of a contemporary Pentecost. The altar has been flooded with needy souls, time and time again. Witness is abundant. Release. Freedom. There are tears. Repentance. Joy unspeakable. Embracing. Spontaneous applause when a soul celebrates. A thousand hearts lifted in songs of praise and adoration to a Mighty God.

"Forgiveness. Expressions of hidden guilt and resentments. God is convicting His children. No sheer emotion. No psychology to get people to the altar. Singing. Shouting. The song, *'How Great Thou Art.'* After two and a half hours, hands are in the air. Pointed toward God. A brother and sister at the altar. Friends, couples, roommates at the altar. Another song, *'Turn Your Eyes Upon Jesus.'* My old roommate has found the victory. He is urging other friends to rid themselves of the old trash and garbage that claim their lives.

"Basketball players with their coach at the altar. A girl is singing, *'Broken Pieces'* with these words, 'He is my reason for living.' Black people. White people. God's people. Prayer request for a mother who left God two years ago. A Spanish girl singing, *'He touched me.'* A boy from California says, "Praise God, I've kicked the habit." My roommate has not moved in five hours from his seat. I have seen the hearts of Asburians opened today. Laid bare. A new sense of honesty and integrity. The truth is refreshing. Human pride is a stumbling block."

SEVEN HOURS HAVE PASSED

"A brilliant student is witnessing to the sweetness of his relationship with Christ. He is saying, 'Christ is no longer an option. He is a necessity.' Again, the song, *'How Great Thou Art'* and others like *'Pass me not oh Gentle Savior, hear my humble cry.'* Others sang, *'Just A Closer Walk With Thee.'* A boy sang, *'It Took A Miracle.'* Another sang, *'Without Him.'* Seven hours have passed. Eight hours. Weeping, sobbing, intense prayer. A seminary student yearns for God to move in the (Asbury) Seminary (across the street).

Inside Hughes Auditorium.

Dr. Hanke wrote, "Toward the supper hour, some began to leave, but the building began to fill again as the marathon service entered into the evening. At times, nearly every seat in the 1,500-seat auditorium was occupied. Some people were standing around the walls. Others were looking on from the doorways, sometimes virtually blocking the exits. A sweet, gentle current of the Holy Spirit circulated within the congregation giving a feeling of warmth around the heart.

Chapter Four
PRESIDENT DENNIS KINLAW'S STORY

In all observance of the Asbury College 1970 Revival, God in his providence had placed the right leader in the college just two years before, to understand the movement of God and understand how the Holy Spirit moved in such a miraculous way. His role in the 1970 revival was crucial.

So, one of the most amazing aspects of this historic revival was the fact that when revival came during that Tuesday morning chapel at Asbury, Dr. Kinlaw had departed early that morning for an 8 o'clock flight from Louisville on college business to Calgary Alberta, Canada. It took him all day, and when he arrived at 5 p.m. at his hotel, he was handed an emergency note by the hotel desk clerk. He recognized immediately that it was from Dean Reynolds. Dr. Kinlaw thought of campus uprisings all over the nation that was going on at that time, even president's being locked in their offices. What could possibly have gone wrong at Asbury?

Homer Pointer

"The morning the revival began, I was working on a term paper, so I cut chapel. I went to my 11:00 class, but no one else was there. After lunch, I decided to visit Hughes Auditorium for a little while and see what was happening. My four years at Asbury had really embittered me, especially because of the un-Christian ways we all treated each other. Two of my co-workers on the COLLEGIAN (student newspaper) staff spoke to me about the condition of my spiritual life. I tried to ignore them but not the joy and happiness they possessed that I did not have. Finally, I knelt at the altar to rededicate my life to Christ. The 90 minutes I prayed that afternoon of February 3, has completely revolutionized my life. I learned during the revival to expect a miracle for we have a God who deals in them. I know, because He performed one in my own heart."

∽

Dr. Kinlaw went immediately to a pay telephone, placed a Canadian dime to make the call, and in 30 seconds, got the Dean at his home. It was about 7 o'clock Kentucky time. The Dean said, "I have a problem and don't know quite how to handle it.' My blood pressure rose a little bit, and I said, "What is the problem?" "Well," he said, "it's chapel." I said, "What do you mean, it's chapel?" He said, "Well, it's not over yet." And I said, "Would you repeat that please?" and he said, "The morning chapel isn't over yet." I said, "What do you mean it isn't over yet? It's 7 o'clock at night." He said, "That's right, it isn't over yet." And I said, "What happened?" and then he told me. He was scheduled to speak that morning and instead of speaking, he had given his witness. He never became a Christian until he was an adult. After he had shared his witness, he opened for students to share what Christ was doing in their lives, and what God was saying to them. There was a remarkable response.

"About five minutes before the chapel hour was over, a philosophy professor turned to the Dean who had come down and was sitting on the front row and said. 'God is here. If you give an invitation there will be a response.' He gave an invitation and that started a response that lasted until the next Tuesday morning, a week later when we began classes again."

Dr. Dennis Kinlaw

Then Dean Reynolds told Dr. Kinlaw that the TV news media from Lexington have asked to come in and do a report on the revival. Dr. Kinlaw's first response was that they would be cynical, coming into that sacred place, perhaps making a joke out of it, and thought it not a good idea. However, Dean Reynolds said that they had prayed about it and felt that they should let them in. Dr. Kinlaw reluctantly agreed but said make sure they keep it reverent.

Chapter Five

TUESDAY EVENING 11 P.M. – 13 HOURS HAVE PASSED

In his account, Jeff Blake continues. "Thirteen hours have passed, '*What A Friend We Have in Jesus*' is sung. Thirty-nine people at the altar. Prayers are lifted for churches that are in desperate need of revival. A lovely saxophone is playing '*Take My Hand Precious Lord*' and the congregation joins in singing. Weeping among several people. At midnight, the heart of God must look on Hughes Auditorium with great joy. The Psalmist said, 'I commune with my heart in the night; I meditate and search my spirit' ...Psalm 77:6."

Dr. Hanke remembers, "The classrooms in the basement served as meeting places for special prayer groups or afforded a quiet Bethel for someone to meditate upon heavenly things. It was common to see students seated or kneeling together, two-by-two, with an open Bible praying and discussing the things of God."

WEDNESDAY MORNING – ASBURY SEMINARY ACROSS THE ROAD IS TOUCHED

Across the road from Asbury College is the Asbury Seminary. God was about to move there as well. Dr. Hanke goes on to say, "During the first day, some of the 450 seminary students were deeply moved by the divine visitation on Asbury College and began to yearn for the same spiritual renewal on their campus across the street. An all-night prayer meeting was quickly called. This vigil intensified the burden for revival that some had felt for many months.

∽

Jerry Borelli

"I came to Asbury in 1968 thinking I was a Christian because I did not smoke, swear or drink. I went to church every Sunday so I thought I was 'right' with God. This revival has made me realize that Christianity was not the farce I was. Being a Christian does not mean just kneeling at an altar and ending it there. It is a day-by-day growing process. I had been jealous of the talents of others, their clothes, social status, academic abilities and athletic abilities. But now that I know the Lord better, I can work to achieve better things because 'I can do all things through Christ, which strengthens me.'"

∽

"The next morning at the regular seminary chapel service, it happened. This program, too, was unusual in that no formal preaching was planned. Rather, the time was scheduled as a hymn-sing. When one student stood up to relate how the revival had affected his life, many under the power of the Spirit began to move on the altar. There followed the now-familiar pattern of hearts melting in the refining fire of God's presence.

"Some of the students and faculty came to the pulpit and openly acknowledged faults and spiritual needs. Resentments, hidden jealousies, lustful desires, worldly attitudes of all kinds were brought out into the open. A sin often confessed related to the indifferent way the holy things of God had been treated. As one graduate student expressed it, 'I've become nonchalant about this whole business of being a Christian and of witnessing to others.' Asking for prayers of his associates, he fell at the altar to seek forgiveness and to make a new and deeper surrender of his life.

"The service continued into the afternoon. Some classes tried to meet, but many students remained in the chapel where the divine presence was still so much in evidence. By the next day, all classes were officially cancelled for the rest of the week."

Jeff Blake's account continues with vivid memory of God's mighty presence.

"On Wednesday, February 4, 34 souls were at the altar. Three hundred to 400 people present as this new day dawns. The president of the senior class has been filled with the spirit. Shortly after noon, on this Wednesday; bright skies; a bitterly cold day in the snow, however; a teacher at the college is witnessing. Seven people waiting to witness. Word comes that revival has spread to the seminary."

27 HOURS HAVE PASSED

"At 1:15 p.m., an unusual spirit of holiness at this moment. The altar is flooded with souls, 30 or 40. A soldier who returned recently from Vietnam is speaking. He witnesses to the cleansing of God in his sinful life. A senior from the seminary is speaking. He found release last night in the service."

PRESIDENT KINLAW CONTINUES...

"So, on Wednesday, the TV News came from Lexington, and in the evening report, the newscaster (Billy Thompson of WLEX-TV) began in an unusual way. "What is happening at Wilmore has touched me more than anything in my 34 years of news reporting. Normally, when you are watching television, you have one eye on television or one ear to someone else in the room; perhaps you are fixing the evening meal. But for the next two and a half minutes, I wish you would stop everything that you are doing, and I think that you too are going to be impressed.

"It started at ten o'clock yesterday morning. Chapel was scheduled to end at eleven o'clock yesterday morning. It

didn't end at eleven o'clock yesterday morning, it didn't end at eleven o'clock last night, it didn't end at eleven o'clock this morning, in fact, as Jim and I took to the air, it was still going on. Let's have a look and a listen." That news report was the beginning of many, and God used the media to spread the word across America. In fact, during the week of revival, hundreds of people made their way to Asbury College to see the mighty move of God and be touched themselves by the power of God that was present.

For Dr. Kinlaw in Canada, all he knew about the revival was through the telephone. He recalled a moving moment in a telephone booth. "I will never, ever forget, standing in a public telephone booth a day later as I called to find out what was taking place. If you are not a Christian, you wouldn't understand this. If you have had a sense of the presence of God, you will understand this. In all of my life, I have never known a heavier sense of the presence of God than in that small telephone booth, standing beside a roadway in Alberta, Canada. It was as if God himself came through the telephone line. And I was encompassed in God.

"Now part of my reaction to the revival was almost fear. There was an apprehension in me, less anything be done you know to grieve the Spirit. And also, the question, was I worthy in any sense to be a part of any of that? And could I respond as I ought to. There was a deep intense consciousness that we were dealing with holy things, sacred things even though I was far removed.

Chapter Six
THURSDAY MORNING – 48 HOURS HAVE PASSED

"On Thursday, February 5, fresh snow fell on the earth on this particular day in Wilmore," Jeff Blake continued to journal. "Even as God was making all things new in His creation, He was moving actively in the lives of people in Hughes Auditorium, in dorm rooms, all over the Asbury campus. Forty-eight hours have passed. Almost 1,500 people here in Hughes. The altar is filled. Several people are waiting to give their witnesses. A marvelous sight. Supernatural. This is the way God planned it." *'Amazing Grace,' 'All Hail the Power of Jesus Name,' 'Great Is Thy Faithfulness'* are sung as witnesses continued and with the altar overflowing.

Arthur L. Lindsay of the Asbury Public Relations Office, in a later report to the Asbury alumni, made this statement after two days of revival on Thursday, "From around the nation and across the world have come requests for prayer. Most noteworthy of these have been more than a dozen other Christian colleges in the United States, who have both promised prayer support for a similar meeting of God's Spirit on their campus.

"There, of course, is no way of telling how long the meeting will continue, but as of ten o'clock on Thursday morning, there is no sign of letup. There have been no classes on the Asbury campus in two days, and there will be none at least on Thursday. In addition to this, the basketball games regularly scheduled for Thursday evening have been postponed."

PRESIDENT KINLAW – 2:30 A.M. FRIDAY MORNING

"I didn't get back to the campus until early Friday morning. I landed in Louisville about 12 o'clock on Thursday night. I got in my automobile and drove to Wilmore. I had read accounts of (Charles) Finney's relating of the revivals in his day. When Finney would go into a city sometime, people would come under a profound sense of the presence of God. The closer I got to Wilmore the heavier that sense of God got on me. When I drove my car at 2:30 in the morning to the campus, I didn't go home, I went to the auditorium and I parked. As I came up the steps, I walked very slowly. I didn't know what I was walking into, but I knew it was the presence of God. You don't do that casually. I walked very slowly up the steps and walked on in.

"Now in a small college of 1,000 -1,100 students, which we had, a President is something of a 'Papa figure.' He's the authority symbol. He's the leader. When I walked in, I knew that many of those young people would be waiting for me. And the question was, what was my role to be in it? Was I to go to the platform? Was I, the President, to involve myself? I walked in and sat in the back corner seat as far away from the center as I could get, but still where I could see what was going on. There was that awesome sense of the presence of God, and I did not want to be an unclean instrument or presence in any of it. I sat there for I suppose an hour.

James Davis

"Prior to the revival, I had been growing in my Christian experience, and yet my prayer life was zero. I could not reach God. There was no power in my life. From the outset of the revival, I was skeptical. I couldn't get excited and I couldn't feel anything at all. I knew something was missing. After a three-day struggle, I went to the altar to seek what God had for me. I still do not know what it was, but it met my need completely. Now, I know what it means to be a disciple of Christ and not just a follower. I know that I do matter to God."

∽

"A format had been developed. It started in that opening chapel. A student would give his witness and tell about how God was dealing with him and the sin in his life. He'd make a confession and tell how God had brought forgiveness to him, restoration or how the spiritual need of his heart had been met. As he would speak, someone in the audience would speak and say, 'That's like me.' That person would come under conviction, come forward and kneel at the altar.

"So a pattern had been developed of testimony, and after the testimony, prayer and singing and praise and adoration. And then, more witnessing and sharing of how God had met human need. So, as I sat there, I heard these students sharing what God was doing in their hearts how their lives had been cleaned out. Some were saying that God was restoring them after they had known Him before, and others would tell how for the first time they had found Him. Others shared how relationships had been straightened out.

"I suppose I had been there an hour when a young lady spotted me and she came up to where I was sitting. She knelt beside me and looked up and said, "Dr. Kinlaw, may I talk with you?" I said, "Why yes." She said, "I need help...I am a liar." (Note: Dr. Kinlaw broke with emotion as he recounted this episode.) I could tell she wanted to talk privately, so we walked downstairs and sat down in a class room.

"She looked at me and I looked at her and she said, 'Dr. Kinlaw, I am a liar. I lie so much, I don't even know when I'm lying. I am a liar. Now what do I do?' Then Dr. Kinlaw recalls his thoughts. "Well, I sat there for a moment or two, and I had never said this to anybody else. But I looked at her and I said, 'Why don't you start back to the last person you remember that you lied to. Confess it to that person, and ask him or her to forgive you."

"Oh," she said, "That would kill me." I said, "No, it would probably cure you. Three days later, she came to me radiant, and she said, 'Dr. Kinlaw, I'm free!' I said, "What do you mean, you're free?" She said, 'I just hit my 34th person, and I'm free." Now that was the kind of thing that was taking place, an honest, candid dealing with personal sin, personal disobedience and personal problems.

"It was marvelous the way these young people would respond. And at night, you would see students lined up by the telephones in the dormitories ready to call their families or friends about the revival." They would call at night because of the cheaper rates.

Dr. Kinlaw told of one student named Susan who got on the telephone to call her Dad, a close friend of Dr. Kinlaw's, who served in The Salvation Army in New York City. They didn't have much money and they had a family agreement that Susan wouldn't call home except for an emergency. When her parents answered the phone, her Dad said, "Susan, what is the emergency?" Susan said, "Well, Dad, I've called to tell you some good news. Today, I found Jesus!" The Salvation Army officer said, "What do you mean, you've found Jesus. Honey, you've known Jesus for years." Susan said, "No, Dad, I've never known Jesus before. Today, I found Jesus." He said, "Honey, you have been in street meetings with me, you've run youth camps, you've witnessed up and down this part of this country. You've been in the Army all your life. What do you mean, you have found Jesus?"

Susan said, "Apparently, you don't understand." He said, "What were you doing all these years?" She said, "Dad, I wasn't doing those things because I loved Christ. I was doing those things because I loved you. I wanted to please you, but today, I found Jesus." He's a personal friend of mine and his response then was, "What's that Kinlaw guy trying to do down there?" That was the only time anyone tried to relate anything that was going on there to me. About two weeks later, her parents went to a service in Connecticut where she was witnessing and that Salvation Army officer said, 'Yes, she's right, she had found Jesus.'"

Dr. Kinlaw shared an overall view of what was taking place non-stop in Hughes Auditorium. "There was an amazing openness and transparency. There was a kind of thing that terrifies administrators. It, you know, is the kind of thing that drives you batty. You have a microphone up here and students lined up and you don't have the foggiest notion of what one of them is going to say and you don't have the foggiest notion of what one of them is going to do and you are responsible for some decorum or some rationality in all of that, you see. So, you sit with your heart in your throat while you watch all of this.

"It was amazing the restraint of the Holy Spirit. The emphasis was never upon the need for restitution; the need was to repair human relationships, human being to human being, and the need for bringing a life to the highest and the best."

On Friday, February 6, revival has spread to other Christian campuses. Requests are coming in from colleges, seminaries and churches for students to come where they are, tell them about the Asbury Revival and how God is moving in an unusual way. "This revival is taking a national form. Prayers for a youth rally in Norfolk, Virginia," says Blake. "Students are flying and driving to places where the requests have come in.

"One reporter asked the president (Dr. Dennis Kinlaw) on the telephone how this revival began. He responded, 'It is just as though Jesus walked in and He has never left.

Chapter Seven
FRIDAY 10:30 P.M. – 84 HOURS HAVE PASSED

"At 10:30 p.m., *'And Can It Be'* was sung. Forty-two souls at the altar. Teachers are witnessing of their faith in God. I have just seen a couple rise from the altar after three and one-half hours of prayer. They are victorious. The laying on of hands at the altar. Intense sobbing at one end of the altar. A lovely young lady walked to the microphone and said, 'For the glory of God,' and sang beautifully *'The Battle Hymn Of The Republic.'* I wish you could have heard it, especially when 1,500 other voices sang in the night. Oh, how glorious. Hands outstretched in the air. Overwhelming. I am simply overcome with the joy of the moment.

"An urgent need for missionaries. Incredible need. Near midnight, I see a girl in the very last seat, high in the balcony. Her head is bowed low in a deep spirit of prayer. Serenity. Peace. The answer to the needs of the world. An utter peace. The peace of God which passeth all understanding."

"Sometimes songs would break out spontaneously. By evening, people began to come from off-campus with some reporting they were overcome with conviction of sin as they came on campus." Word spread fast. A Lexington, KY television station was permitted to come and report what they saw. The newscaster was a Christian and joyously reported what was happening at Asbury.

~

> *"In February, I received the baptism of the Holy Spirit. To paraphrase the words of Hosea, the Holy Spirit came and brought us joy that overflowed like the spring rains that water the earth. I found the secret of a victorious life. Not always happy and not always on the mountaintop, but I have victory over every day circumstances and frustrations that plague the life of every human. I'm grateful and I thank the name of Jesus Christ that I don't have to spend another day of my life without the reality of Jesus Christ in my life and without the power of the Holy Spirit." Female student witness....*

~

I asked Jeannine what was her reaction after two and a half years of earnest prayer for Revival on the campus. "I just stood in the back of the auditorium laughing, rejoicing and just overwhelmed with joy. I witnessed the power of prayer like never before. It was glorious. Deep holy awe enveloped me. How can I begin to tell what it was like to have the manifest presence of God in our midst. God had given us His supreme gift…Himself. We were riveted in our seats. Time evaporated. What seemed like just a few minutes, actually, it was hours.

"You just couldn't leave. I didn't go to my room until 5 a.m. the next morning, slept only three hours and returned by 8 a.m. The power of God came down. God was in the room. In fact, for the entire seven days, I probably ate only seven meals and slept only 20 hours. You just didn't want to leave and miss anything like this, and you had no way of knowing how long it would last."

Arthur L. Lindsay, in his report said, "It is really impossible to tell just when the school will return to its regular schedule. But, school officials intend that as long as the revival is purposive, they will not do anything to hinder the continuing movement of the Spirit of

God. Three straight days, with no let-up in the process of singing, praying, testifying, and fresh commitments to Jesus Christ, is a record in intensity of this sort of happening. Men and women who were present for similar revivals in 1950 and 1958 attest that this revival is deeper and more intense that either of those."

Stevens also recalls, "The Presence of God was so public and so 'thick' that some students went so far as to join forces against responding to Christ, making pacts not to go to Hughes Auditorium. Others would awaken from sleep and rush to the altar to find Christ. One student stood at the podium reporting the concern of his heart that one of his roommates would find the Lord. That very roommate walked into the auditorium and headed straight to the altar. The student speaking was visibly moved and left the podium to pray with his roommate."

"Day after day, the campus community was absorbed in only one thing - getting right with God and seeking His will," Dr. Hanke wrote. "Divine prerogatives transcended all other considerations. Being present at the services seemed to be the most important thing at the moment. Radio, TV, parties, ball games and other activities did not hold any appeal. One person was heard to say, 'I have gone on a complete radio and TV fast.' Time did not seem to matter. Many students were so engrossed in the Spirit that they stayed in the chapel a better part of the whole week.

"Occasionally, the pattern of witnessing was interrupted by special seasons of prayer in response to the many need of revival requests coming in. Telegrams, letters and phone calls contained urgent appeals for prayer from all over the United States and Canada. Reports of the revival outreach in other communities were shared from time to time. When the news of some new victory was heard, people would break forth into shouts of praise while the congregation would pick up on the strains of the organ and with uplifted hands would join in singing, '*To God be the Glory*.'

"Hundreds of visitors were attracted to the campus through news reports of the revival. Some came as far away as California, Florida and Canada. Many were greatly stirred by the Holy Spirit and came to the platform to testify of their renewal. A couple intended to stop for a short visit and stayed a week. Another car full of people were on their way to spend a vacation in West Virginia with relatives, but they were so overcome with the revival spirit that they spent all of their vacation in Asbury."

Numbers for the revival peaked on Friday night at 10 p.m. with approximately 1,600 people packing Hughes Auditorium that seats 1,500.

Chapter Eight

SATURDAY MORNING – 96 HOURS HAVE PASSED

In Jeff Blake's account, he writes that on Saturday morning, February 7, the altar is flooded with seekers at 8:20 a.m. Prayers for the administration, the professors. Beautiful singing. Over a 1,000 here on this winter morning. At 8:40 a.m., the president (Dr. Dennis Kinlaw) is urging a long view of these days we have spent in the presence of God. He speaks to us out of the 55th chapter of Isaiah, 'Ho, everyone who thirsts, come to the waters; and he who has no money, come, buy and eat!'

∼

Nancy Chadwell

"To God be the glory…great things He has done!" So many times, I have sung this song without fully realizing what truly great things the Lord can do. He has given me a love for others that I never knew possible. After I took my eyes off people and focused them on Christ, He was able to show me deeper things, which He had in store for me. It is as if Jesus and I have become personal friends instead of casual acquaintances."

"In these past days, there is a sense that God has separated us from the world and shut the world out so that He could speak. God has our attention. God wants us. We are involved in a purpose. A mission. We must be a flying wedge in a pagan society. God wants to get us ready. What is God getting us ready for? Let us walk seriously, meekly, obediently.

"For 96 hours now, God has been moving. God makes things real to us through His Spirit. The urgency of meeting God. Students from other colleges in this section of our nation are here. I see a whole group of students from a visiting college as they weep for revival on their campus. Many are coming in tonight from various states. We are not concerned with showing people where Asbury is, but we are concerned with showing people the Christ served by Asburians. Into a dying and lost world, we must go."A professor from the University of Kentucky is witnessing at 11:15 p.m.; 700 to 800 people in Hughes. I don't know that I've ever seen the altar area so crowded. As Saturday faded into Sunday, I remember the singing of *All Hail the Power of Jesus Name*. He is being crowned. Hallelujah!"

Chapter Nine
SUNDAY MORNING – 120 HOURS HAVE PASSED

Sunday, the Sabbath Day, proved to be an unusual day at Asbury. Jeannine Brabon remembers, "There were probably no more than 300 or 400 students on campus. All other students were spread out across the country telling people about the revival from the many requests we received. Yet, there was standing room only in Hughes Auditorium, more than 1,600 people. Local Asbury churches dismissed their regular services and encouraged their people to go to the revival."

Dr. Hanke describes what happened as Wilmore churches united in worship. "One of the most moving hours of the week came that morning when one of the local pastors took his place at the pulpit and poured out his agonized soul and confessed his shortcomings. He was followed by his wife who confessed at length her unhappy state of mind about being a pastor's wife in Wilmore. Both testified to a renewal of grace and an infilling of divine love. The pastor called several people by name and made his peace with them.

"The president (Dr. Kinlaw) of Asbury College suggested that there should be more than 100 adults among the faculty, staff and town community who should come to the altar and make things right with God and man. Immediately, a mass of people moved forward, filling the front section of the auditorium and front aisles. Many prayed and wept with deep emotion, and afterward, came to the platform to make apologies to those whom they had wronged and against whom they had resentment. The spiritual and social healing which occurred on that Sunday morning has solved more problems than any other event in the town for many years.

MONDAY AND TUESDAY – 168 HOURS HAVE PASSED

In his report to the alumni, Lindsay wrote that through the weekend, invitations had come from across America for students to share the revival movement. "At latest count, the students had gone to 16 different states to participate in church services, college chapels and convocations. An estimated 400 to 500 young people out of a student body of 1,000 had gone out in such endeavors.

"Another development in the nationwide extension of the Asbury revival has been the formation of the College Prayer Net on shortwave radio. Sixteen colleges from coast-to-coast joined the program which aired at 5:00 p.m. Wilmore time."

"The spontaneous revival continued on Monday into the chapel period on Tuesday, February 10. Many were still in line to give their witness. Some had appeared before the congregation several times, giving progress reports on their own spiritual development or reporting how God had worked through their witness."

Lindsay wrote, "The pattern was the same as it had been since the start a week ago: singing, praying, testifying and new decisions on the altar. At the conclusion of the period, those who were waiting to testify agreed to return in the evening; the several at the altar continued to pray."

WEDNESDAY 3 A.M. – THE LAST STUDENT LEFT HUGHES AUDITORIUM - 185 HOURS HAVE PASSED

Dr. Hanke describes the last hours this way. "The administration decided to resume classes at the end of the period (Tuesday morning chapel). However, the auditorium was kept open for prayer and an agreement was made to have a nightly meeting. Students continued to come and go throughout the day and into the night. Shortly after 3 a.m. on Wednesday morning, the last student left the sanctuary. For 185 hours---without any interruption---the services had continued! During all this time, there was no pressure, no scheduled meetings, no paid advertising, no offering, no preaching, no invocation, no prelude or postlude, and no benediction.

"And no one tried to compile any statistics. It was felt that this would be out of keeping with the spirit of the revival, but most of the students on campus of the college and seminary knelt at the altar, and there were thousands of other persons who made a similar dedication. The whole spiritual tone of the campus was completely changed.

∽

"As a missionary from India, 16 years just prior to coming here, we have seen some wonderful, miraculous movements of the Spirit there. But I have never witnessed anything like this, the sheer awesome power of God in our midst."

…An Asbury professor

∽

"The lights in the Hughes Auditorium still have not been turned out. Even now, months later, a few people gather each evening to pray, witness and rejoice together. Often these meetings last into the midnight hours, with visitors frequently being helped on to God. Also, during most hours of the day, someone may still be seen entering the chapel. They kneel to pray for a few minutes, then leave. Others just sit and stare at the altar so ripe with precious memories. If one looks closely, tears may be seen coursing down their cheeks."

Lindsay added more insights after seven days of revival. "Even though classes resumed on Tuesday, the revival is continuing unabated. Students returning to campus from all over the United

States are reporting great numbers of decisions for Jesus Christ. School officials estimate the number of decisions, both here and elsewhere since the start of the revival, to be in the thousands." School officials made no attempt to tabulate decisions since "it would be out of the spirit of the meeting to try to put it into a statistical mode." A large map of the United States was hung in the foyer of Hughes Auditorium with colored pins indicating towns and states where students had gone.

Chapter Ten

TEARS CONTINUE TO FLOW INTO POST REVIVAL

"Perhaps tears express more eloquently than words what had happened. There is no human vocabulary that can capture the full dimension of one divine moment. In some ways, it seems almost a dream, yet it happened. We saw it with our own eyes. In a way impossible to describe. God was in our midst. Those of us who were there can never look upon the things of this world quite the same," wrote Dr. Hanke.

How remarkable that professor Dr. Howard Hanke and student Jeff Blake had the presence of mind to write such descriptive accounts of this powerful visitation of God on the Asbury campus that February wintry week in 1970. It was as if God spoke to them, maybe unknowingly, to write what they saw and heard. While attending the Asbury Reunion in June of 2019, every alumnus I spoke with, who witnessed and experienced this movement of God as a student, spoke with a quick reflective smile, teary eyes, spontaneous joy and an immediate sense of reverence toward God. The first student I spoke to in the lobby of Hughes Auditorium before the Friday evening Hymn Sing that led off Reunion Weekend, was Steller Keener, a Wilmore resident, who was a sophomore during the revival.

. . .

I asked Steller, "What comes to mind when you think of the 1970 Asbury revival?" "The whole town shut down," said Steller spontaneously. "For two days, I left (the Hughes Auditorium) only to eat. Students lined the aisles giving their testimonies. I realized that I didn't have one. I thought I was a Christian but I found Jesus here." Such would be the story of many Asbury students that week. Freshmen, sophomores, juniors and seniors would be in their early 70's now, but speak as if the revival was a lifetime milestone in that special 'Divine Moment' week.

Chapter Eleven

THE TIM PHILPOT STORY – ONE STUDENT'S AMAZING ACCOUNT

One of the most engaging student testimonies for this historic movement of God came from a freshman named Tim Philpot. He had been on campus only five months. The revival would be life changing for Tim. "I had an unusual childhood. My dad was an evangelist. I do not recall any decision about going to college. It was a given that I would go to Asbury, the college responsible for my own parents' salvation in the late 40's.

"My dad was on the Board at Asbury in 1970. The Philpot name seemed to give me an advantage at Asbury as I entered as a freshman in the fall of 1969. I was a typical teen. I had played the 'Christian' game enough to convince my parents that I was saved and on my way to heaven. But the reality was quite different. I had zero relationship with God. I was a fake, as I told it later.

"As I awoke on February 3, 1970, I had already decided to skip chapel that day. That was because I had been to Alabama the night before to watch the University of Kentucky play basketball at Auburn. My dad was good friends with Coach Adolph Rupp, and he had arranged an excursion for some of his friends. We arrived back in Lexington in the early morning hours of February 3.

"When I got to class at 11 a.m., not a soul was there. I seriously wondered if Jesus had come and I was the only one left behind at this holy place. I wandered over to Hughes Auditorium. It was full. I found a seat in the back. I watched silently for hours. I recall an older teacher, Mrs. Westerfield, saying to me, 'Isn't this wonderful?' I agreed, continuing to fake my Christian experience.

"I was mesmerized, as was everyone, by the experience. No one left. The real action was around the altar, but the entire auditorium was full of reverent talk and prayer. It seemed that God had walked into the room. It was not a question of whether to believe; it was more like watching a movie. What would happen next?

"The main memory about the first days are certain songs. *There's a Sweet, Sweet Spirit in This Place,* was the primary musical memory. It seemed to capture the essence of what was happening. It was a place of forgiveness. Honesty abounded. People confessed sins publicly. Many were more honest than I wanted to hear. I have a vivid memory of pastor David Seamands, probably on Sunday, standing to confess sins himself. Same for a professor named Jim Shepherd.

"I recall thinking that people at their age and position had surely gotten over 'sin' by now. It was shocking. Looking back, I was living in an 18-year-old's delusion that older 'saints' had overcome sin to the point of not needing any more salvation.

"On Thursday night at about 10 p.m., the revival had been going about 60 hours. I was sitting in the back and realized it was time for me to do something. By midnight I had the courage to do something, not knowing what that something should be. I stood and walked back to the entrance hall. I stopped a friend and said, 'I know you may not believe this, but I am not even a Christian.' Her response was to smile and say, 'That's no surprise. In fact, there are five guys downstairs praying for you right now.' She let me know clearly but nicely that I had been fooling no one.

"I vaguely recall walking down the right center aisle to kneel and pray. I was immediately surrounded by a dozen or more people. I have zero recollection of who was there. Steve Seamands may have been there.

"I specifically recall only two things. One, there was a fellow freshman who, for no good reason, I disliked. He was some sort of 18-year-old juvenile rival. As I got up from the altar, I kissed him on the cheek and told him I loved him. And second, but related to the first, was my overall sense of Love that had entered the picture for me. I literally loved everyone. Hatred and jealousy and all the negative emotions about other people completely vanished.

"Looking back, I know the Asbury revival in 1970 had one simple and primary lesson for me; the God of the Bible is to be *experienced*, not just believed. The 1970 revival was not a time of 'decision,' meaning a logical and well-thought-out process to decide to follow Christ. Instead, the revival was an illogical, unplanned event, which proved God goes way beyond our logical ability to figure Him out."

Tim Philpot 1970s

Tim Philpot went all over America in 1970 telling his story of the Asbury revival. His own brother and dozens of teenagers had life changing experiences with God at his Tates Creek High School in Lexington, when revival came there. Says Tim, "I never had notes or a script when I spoke of the revival and shared my testimony. God always helped me tell the story in a unique way. God always showed up." Such was the thrilling story of an Asbury student that was like so many others on campus that week.

Chapter Twelve

A BIBLE PROFESSOR'S CONFESSION IN CHAPEL

Among those who would come to the platform and tell of how God had worked in his life was a professor in the religion department. He spoke in chapel to the student body and faculty a short time after the seven-day visitation of God had ended and classes had resumed. He was young and hadn't been at the college for many years. In his suit and tie at the platform in Hughes Auditorium, he began by saying that he "had come to know Jesus Christ as his personal Savior 13 years before in the military. For about a year, I lived in the grace and knowledge of the Lord. It was a blessed time. Although he was my Savior, I never came to the point that He was Lord of all. That's a dangerous position to be in. Either, he is Lord of all or none at all eventually, and that's what happened to me.

"I began to drift away from the Lord after coming out of the service. The guilt built up and the self-condemnation built up. A burden began to press heavier and heavier about me. And in this backslidden state, I came back here as a student, went through three years, graduated, left here, went to graduate school and I eventually came back on the other side of the desks. I was still in a backslidden state and no longer had a living union with Jesus Christ. I no longer had anything spiritual in the Bible day-by-day. I was living on past experiences and living on past spiritual insights. In spiritual language, I was a hypocrite. The guilt and the condemnation continued to build up. It was heavy and then God came down on February third.

"I knew God was here even in my backslidden state. I even rejoiced on occasion. But at night in my office, I would pray and seek the Lord and I knew I wasn't right. I didn't have the courage to admit it before the student body and my fellow faculty members. Until we humble ourselves, God can't do much for us. I dealt with this the entire week, and then a week later, on February 10 (the following Tuesday), God gave me the grace, and I thank him for it. He gave me the grace to acknowledge my sin and hypocrisy before this body. And when he gave me the grace to humble myself, and acknowledge my need, he met that need.

"And he took the guilt away, the self-condemnation away and the burden away, and gave me a peace, a joy and presence that I don't want to lose again. I praise Him for it. Great Things He has done, is doing and is going to do if we obey and follow the Lord." His was a mighty transformation as a faculty member that once again backed up how God convicted so many of their sins and hypocrisy and made things right with Him.

For years as Dr. Kinlaw would address audiences about the 1970 Asbury Revival, he would tell that story. He would say, "When you have a doctorate in Bible, who would stand up before a whole student body, look at his students and say, 'I have a confession to make. I have cheated you students because I have not properly prepared for my classes. I have gone into classes not as well prepared as I should be, and I stand here today to ask you to forgive me. Now I count that as revival. It is interesting in that his life was transformed, a doctorate in Bible, and he would share that with you. For years later, you could tell a freshness and a sweetness and a presence of God in his life in a very beautiful way. Now that's the way God moved through that week."

Chapter Thirteen

REVIVAL SPREAD ACROSS AMERICA – "THE LESS IMPRESSIVE THE STUDENT WAS, THE MORE EFFECTIVE AN INSTRUMENT HE WAS"

There is a second part to the 1970 Asbury Revival that is just as thrilling as what took place that week on campus. Dr. Kinlaw related, "By Friday, when I returned, the word (of the Revival) had spread all across the country. In fact, before the week was out, one of our students was on the west coast sharing in a Christian college what happened. Another student was on the east coast. That weekend, after it began on Tuesday, our students were all over the United States and in Canada.

"Now, what I thought was that God had turned something over in their souls. He had been so good that they had to share it and they started out, going back to their home and other places. What was more impressive was that by Thursday, we began to get calls from all over the United States and Canada saying, 'We'll be glad to pay the way of a group of students to tell us what's taking place there.' And so students went from the east coast to the west coast, the Gulf of Mexico and Canada.

"They were witnessing and speaking in places where no one from Asbury had sought the opportunity or taken the initiative to go there. The Holy Spirit was at work at the other end in hunger. People were saying, 'Would someone come and tell us about it?' One of the most impressive and beautiful things to me was the way the Holy Spirit worked. There was no preaching during those eight days. There was only sharing and witnessing."

"And the amazing thing was that as a person would tell what had happened, it would be recapitulated. As a person would go somewhere and tell what God had done in Hughes Auditorium, it would take place in the church where the person was telling it. I had a friend who was a college pastor of the Church of the Nazarene, and he was having a revival. He had an evangelist and a quartet that was singing that night, and their service was on the radio. About a quarter of eight before the service began, one of the ushers came in and said to him, there are two students out here from Asbury College and they said they wanted to talk with you. They said that revival has broken out at Asbury.

"And he said, 'Oh, bring them in.' Don said he was standing there with his evangelist and quartet and he looked at these two students. He said they weren't impressive looking, but there they stood and looked at him and he said, 'Yes?' And they said, 'We're from Asbury College. God has come to Asbury and He told us to come tell you that He had been to Asbury and that He wanted to come to your college.' And that was all they said and he said, 'Oh. Well that's wonderful. So, what do you do?' And somewhere or the other, they suggested that they share in the evening service.

"He had never laid eyes on these two boys before. He wasn't about to turn his pulpit over to them. He didn't know what they would do. And they said, 'Oh, that's not our problem. Our problem was to do what He told us to do, and we've done it and we're clean.' So my pastor friend said, 'Well, maybe you should tell us about it. Could you do it in five minutes?' They said, 'Oh, we don't have to do it. We've done what we were told to do.'"

My pastor friend said, 'Let's take five minutes.' So they sang a number and he said, 'We have two students here from Asbury

College. They tell us that God has come to the campus of Asbury College and they want to tell us about it. So they took their coats off, and they were in their shirt sleeves. That was sort of offensive to me. Remember that was 1970." He said, "Nevertheless, the first one stood up and said, 'In Chapel Tuesday, the Holy Spirit came to the Asbury campus. He touched our hearts and our lives. We're different. Our campus is different and we've just come to tell you what He has done for us.'

"He sat down and the pastor told me, 'He may have taken a minute and forty seconds. The second student stood up and in less than about four minutes, both of them had finished what they were going to say.' Then the pastor told me, 'I sighed in relief and I thought, well that's over with.' Unless you are a preacher, you won't understand that, but if you are a preacher, you do understand that. So he said, now we can get on with the service.

"So, he introduced the quartet and the quartet sang one verse and before they moved into the second verse, a member of the quartet, I think it was the bass, raised his hand and stopped them and said, 'God has spoken to me. I need Him to do for me what those guys said that He has done for them. He walked out of the pulpit, left his quartet, got down on his knees at the altar and at ten o'clock that night, there were more people in that church than there were at eight. And revival ran through the night."

Dr. Kinlaw made a great observation about the students as they went out to share. "It was almost the less impressive the student was, the more effective an instrument he was." He gave another example of a young female student. "One little girl was so shy, if she told you her name, she would blush. She went home and on Sunday, she spoke in five churches. If my memory is correct, I think there were 200 people that responded."

"Where the story was told, it was like a spark going from a fire hitting dry brush and it would break out. Now it spread that way to campuses, to churches. It crossed denominational lines. Most of us at Asbury are United Methodists. The revival probably had a larger numerical impact in the Southern Baptist Convention than it did in the United Methodist Church. One student went to Southwestern Baptist Seminary and revival broke out in a classroom. It was a work of God."

Chapter Fourteen

REVIVAL REFLECTIONS FROM PRESIDENT KINLAW

Dr. Kinlaw made another interesting observation. "It was interesting how the media responded to this Revival. They didn't all respond alike. I remember one newspaper reporter called me and said, 'You call this a spontaneous revival?,' and I said yes. He said, 'Now really what you mean is, haven't you had these kind of things before?' I said yes, we have over a period of years. He said, 'What you mean is that you have a group on campus who said, now we haven't had a spontaneous revival in a long time. We better have one, hadn't we?' I said, 'Sir, we have a group of people like that on campus all the time, but they don't seem to be able to produce it.' He said, 'Well, sir, how do you account for this?' I said, 'I would suspect this would be difficult for you, but the only way I know how to explain it is that last Tuesday morning, Jesus walked into Hughes Auditorium and He's been here ever since. And a community is paying tribute to His presence.'

"And that's the way we felt about it. I couldn't get my wife to stay home and cook meals. You couldn't get her out of Hughes Auditorium. If Jesus physically, literally came to your campus, you would forget everything, too. And that's the way we were. You couldn't keep us out of Hughes Auditorium. There is where the Holy Presence was.

"You say, Okay, how did it come? What caused it? No question in my mind was our need. We needed it a lot worse than anybody else around. God honors need and has infinite mercy. And another thing, we had some students who were interested in prayer. One young lady (Jeannine Brabon) became deeply concerned for the blessing of God upon our campus. So she gathered a group around her and they started praying.

"In October, before the Spirit came in February, six students banded together in what they called 'The John Wesley Great Experiment.' They covenanted for 30 days to take 30 minutes in prayer, the Word and writing down the Truth they got from the Word that they were to obey that day, sharing their faith somewhere in the course of the day. Then they met once each week in the course of those 30 days, checking up on each other to see if each one had done his disciplines that week.

"So, for 30 days, they met that way. At the end of that 30 days, we came toward the end of the fall term. At the beginning of the winter term, each one of those six picked up five people. So now there were six groups of six that were getting up every morning for 30 minutes extra to pray and spend time with God. That experience ended on the 31st of January. On that day, they had the Chapel and there were 36 of them on the platform. And the 36 shared what that 'Great Experiment' had done for them. And they had placed in every seat of the auditorium, a commitment slip, and they asked every student in the student body to commit himself or herself, and become a part of a group of six. That was for just 30 days.

"That was on Saturday, the 31st of January. In some ways, that was the most impressive Chapel I ever saw at Asbury. The students shared what time with God had done for them. The next Chapel was Tuesday, the 3rd of February. In addition to this, the young lady (Jeannine Brabon) had gone to proper authorities and asked for a place of prayer. They would meet for prayer and then they started having night prayer meetings. They called an all-night prayer meeting in Hughes Auditorium and a large group gathered around the altar.

"Now here is the way they worked. They were praying for God to come. And when they would finish a prayer meeting, they would look at each other and say, 'Do you think He will come today?' It takes students doesn't it? It takes young people doesn't it? They'd finished their prayer meeting and look at each other and say, do you think He will come today?

"At that all-night prayer meeting on October 3, and I think somewhere around 2:30, they called each other together, stood around the altar, held hands and said, 'That's enough, He's coming.' They went to their rooms and went to bed, and He did come four months later. Now out of all the experiences that Elsie and I ever had, we had never known anything like that. And the things that we find ourselves yearning for now is to see it again.

"I came to the place deep in my heart, you know every generation of students ought to have a chance to see that once. And I believe that God wants to do it again and I believe there is a stirring, some moving, and I think it will depend upon you and me. If I understand what God has done here and what the students here feel, they seem to be saying that we have found together, God can make bad people good, the best of people better. That power is found in Jesus Christ.

"We know that we have found an answer. We believe that it is the answer to the need of the heart of man, both corporately and individually. That after new life in Christ, through repentance for sin, faith in a living Christ, and immediate obedience to His holy will, Jesus is the answer and we commend that to you."

Chapter Fifteen

FOR MONTHS, STUDENTS SHARE, AND REVIVAL BREAKS OUT IN SCHOOLS ACROSS AMERICA

As Dr. Kinlaw stated, by Friday requests were coming in from across America requesting students to come and tell the story of what was taking place at Asbury College. Henry James, publicity director at Asbury, says "With the dispatch of these witnesses, the local revival began to take on the dimensions of a national movement. By summer of 1970, at least 130 colleges, seminaries and Bible schools had been touched by the revival outreach, and witnesses continue to go to other schools and local churches."

French professor Anna Gulick, 51, was teaching at Asbury College in 1970. Of the revival, she wrote, "Again and again different ones testified to having been given an overwhelming love for people they just 'couldn't stand' before. School as usual was totally out of the question. If classes had tried to meet, teachers could not have taught or students studied. We could not talk of anything but God and the work He was doing. Somehow word spread, by phone, by letter, by word of mouth.

"For the first several days, it was next to impossible to get a long distance line out of Wilmore, and the electronic static was filled with references to 'God,' the 'Holy Spirit,' and 'Revival.' Now the most recent report I have is that something like 1,500 witness teams have, through June, visited some 135 universities and states, and have gone into hundreds of churches and public high schools across the nation."

As the witnessing teams went out, "the students' approach was simple, yet powerful," says Henry James. "They described the details of the revival story and witnessed of a fresh, personal encounter with God. They told how God had delivered them from their hang-ups and 'turned them on.' Their witness had the ring of reality. Under the anointing of the Holy Spirit, their words became like spiritual darts which pierced the hearts and minds of the listeners.

Azusa Pacific College near Los Angeles, California was one of the first schools to inquire and ask for a student to be flown to their campus and tell the Asbury revival. The student's name was Wayne Anthony. The night before chapel, the faculty had an all-night prayer meeting. "The speaker of the morning did not preach but simply told what happened at Asbury College and shared how his own life had been affected," says James. "Following the report, the dean of students stood and gently asked if there were 'those in the audience who would like to add depth to their religious experience by getting closer to God.' He asked them to step to the front of the chapel.

"At that moment, 150 students stepped out in mass, moved to the front and made altars out of chairs. This mighty surge of the Holy Spirit brought confessions, tears, restitutions and cleansing power," says James. The movement of God's presence led to classes being cancelled for the day as students gave testimonies, prayed and sang for seven hours. Again, here at Azusa Pacific, students immediately called parents and pastors about what was happening there. Prayer groups came together on campus.

The revival even carried over at the basketball game that night as students yelled "Praise the Lord" when a basket was made. They witnessed to the fans at halftime. Several hundred students went from there to the chapel for a two-hour time of witnessing, praise and Holy Communion. Over the weekend, students spoke in congregations, and revival broke out in the churches. Classes were cancelled on Monday as the movement grew and even spread to Pasadena College. The basketball coach broke down and said to a large group, "I have not been the Christian witness I should have been in front of the men on the team. I have failed them as a Christian. I want God to forgive me. I am a different person."

Another school that was shaken was Greenville College in Greenville, Illinois. Nine Asbury seminary students and one collegian drove through the night in sleet and snow to get to Greenville. Again, the students simply shared what had happened at Asbury, and revival broke out among the students and faculty, and lasted all night. The revival lasted for several days, and later the campus coordinator wrote, "Greenville College will never be the same. The Holy Spirit has blown in gale force through our dorms and classrooms, our faculty and administrative offices, and has settled like a heavenly cloud over the sanctuary of the college church. Teams of students and faculty have been fanning out over the Midwest in weekends of witnessing, and the reports read like the Book of Acts."

A *St. Louis Post-Dispatch* reporter was caught by surprise when he found that the students were not interested in talking current affairs such as Viet Nam and racial injustice. He wrote, "They wanted to talk about what happened to them when they were caught up in a spiritual upheaval that turned the whole college upside down, so to speak, and changed their lives forever. There was nothing pietistic in their attitudes. They were open, friendly, smiling, bright-eyed and as eager to tell about it as students at another college would be to tell about how they won the Big Game. Which, in a sense, they felt they had done."

It should be noted that, as the Greenville College witness teams went out to the churches across Illinois and even Southern

Michigan, the majority of the churches were revitalized. This student-led revival had even penetrated churches that had become spiritually dead for years, but now were alive and caught up in this movement of God with renewed joy and love. The student's fire had rekindled their hearts for God.

Chapter Sixteen

REVIVAL FIRE SPREADS POWERFULLY AND MIRACULOUSLY

It seemed the Holy Spirit was already at work for revival everywhere the students went. Students and faculty at Southwestern Baptist Theological Seminary in Ft. Worth, Texas had been praying for a movement of God on their campus for two years. When a professor simply reported the Asbury revival to his class, Henry James remembers, "Spontaneously, the entire group fell before the Lord in prayer. Confessions, bold intercessions and compassionate pleas for personal and seminary revival poured forth with beautiful liberty." When another professor shared the revival news to his class, the same thing happened.

"An invitation was extended for some Asbury students to come and report firsthand about their experiences. One of those students who went with the witness team recalled how they 'prayed all the way to Texas.' When they arrived on campus, they walked into a prayer meeting in the student center where 40 to 50 students were gathered. They were confessing sins, asking for forgiveness and requesting prayer for each other. One of the students told how he had contemplated suicide, but had found the answer in Christ. The revival was well under way," writes James.

On Sunday, the students shared in several churches, and God moved powerfully. On Monday, in the Scarborough Preaching Chapel on campus, the Asbury students shared for 15 minutes. That resulted in one student after another confessing sins of resentment, bitterness, lust, jealousy and cheating. One young woman stood and said that although she was raised in a preacher's home and was a preacher's wife, it had meant nothing to her. She said, "I've just asked Jesus to come into my heart, and He has." Joy sparkled in her tears as she sat down, converted on the spot.

Another young man who was to graduate in two months, came to the pulpit. He admitted his sin of being dishonest in his studies. "This is eating me up," he sobbed. "I've got to get rid of it. Pray for me." He sank to his knees right there and claimed the cleansing of the Lord. The service continued early into the next day. A crowd of 1,200 couldn't resist hearing all the witnesses, and revival continued for several days all over the campus.

One student said, "We knew what we were seeing, hearing, feeling and thinking was not the product of our imaginations. We were meeting God in all His majesty." One professor wrote, "We found ourselves walking in the sense of reverent awe, our minds racing with questions, our wills painfully adjusting to the demands of what God had wrought; our hearts reaching out in eager desire to tell others; our souls lifting in glorious joy and praise; and our minds experiencing new dimensions of loving adoration of the Lord."

As students went to various colleges in many states, what happened at Asbury College came to all the places where they were requested. Two students went to Olivet Nazarene College in Kankakee, Illinois and one observer said the college, "came unglued" by their witnesses. The president was quoted as saying, "I've seen nothing to compare with it in my 21 years as president."

Revival came to dozens of colleges and seminaries as Asbury students shared the story. Some of the colleges included Houghton (NY); Wheaton (IL); Oral Roberts (OK); Trevecca (TN); John Wesley (NC); Berea (KY); Marion (IN); Huntington (IN); George

Carver (GA); Canadian Bible (Sask.); Seattle Pacific (WA); Ft. Wayne (IN); St. Paul (MN); Central Wesleyan (SC); Taylor (IN); Eastern Mennonite (VA); Spring Arbor (Ml); Canadian Nazarene (Manitoba); Union (TN); Oklahoma Baptist; Roberts Wesleyan (NY); Weyland Baptist (TX); Sue Bennett (KY); George Fox (OR) and Fuller Seminary (CA). As Henry James says, "This was only a few colleges where the Asbury revival spread. Each school had its own version, and the extent of penetration varied. But all were marked by a contagious spirit of honest witnessing."

∽

Tom Phillips

Dr. Tom Phillips, who became director of Billy Graham Crusades worldwide, was a first year student in 1970 at the Southern Baptist Theological Seminary in Louisville, Kentucky. Tom, a Vice-President of the Billy Graham Evangelistic Association today, recalls a group of Asbury College students who came to the Southern campus. "Dr. Louie Drummond was professor of revival and evangelism, and knew we needed help at Southern," says Tom. "It had become 13th in the nation in any graduate program. It was terribly academic, and in the process had lost its soul. He knew we were in an academic environment that had left a lot of spiritual life out.

"He was teaching courses on revival, and he wanted us to understand what God had done at Asbury. He told us that next week a few students from Asbury are going to come, and tell you what God did there. They came and spoke in his classes, and the fire of their revival spread into our hearts. Prior to that, the seminary didn't have any evangelistic or worship teams going out at all, as far as I knew. Nobody prayed. It was like it was an embarrassment to pray. To my chagrin, I would slip under the spiral stairway where there was a small prayer room, and pray when I wanted to. After the Asbury students came and God began to move at Southern, prayer groups came in there by the hundreds in an organized way. Prayer extended to dormitories, homes and wherever students lived. My family was touched.

"And then, another student and I would be among many evangelistic teams who would go to towns and cities and even out of state. We would alternate preaching and doing discipleship training. We had churches where you would give an invitation, and everybody would just flood the front weeping. It all came about when those Asbury students came to our campus. I know that God can seed His movement, and He especially uses young people to do it."

∼

However, one of the greatest movements of God occurred in a church. John Seamands, a student, recalls that three students were led to send 20 news releases of the revival to 20 pastors they knew in their denomination. The pastor of the South Meridian Church of God in Anderson, Indiana was an Asbury alumnus and he received one of the letters. An 80-year old lady got word of the revival and she prompted the pastor to telephone Asbury, and a team was invited.

Students leaving campus to share the revival

An Asbury witness team of four girls and three boys and a senior student at the Asbury Seminary arrived on Saturday afternoon, February 21. They mingled with students in the dormitories and student lounges and invited them to worship at 10:45 a.m. the next morning. All seven of the students witnessed and told the revival story to 500 people gathered for the service. Before the invitation was given, people fled to the altar to pray. God moved in the service that lasted for three hours. A larger crowd showed up for the evening service and the pastor decided that he should have a Monday evening service. One-thousand people crowded into the sanctuary that seated only 750. Three churches buses made 10 trips, bringing college students into the service.

The Asbury students shared their witness that evening and returned back to Asbury for their classes. The pastor sought help from several key business leaders and fellow pastors. They decided to run paid advertisements in the local newspaper, and prepared the church gymnasium for overflow crowds. That evening, 1,400 people filled the sanctuary and gym. The following night, the sanctuary was filled as lives were transformed including an alcoholic, an extremely rebellious student and an outstanding athlete.

Noon meetings then took place in the city hall with some 200 attending. A daily prayer breakfast took place at a downtown hotel. Drawn to these gatherings were businessmen, night-shift workers, housewives and students. High school students began to arrive 30 minutes early for school to pray together. College dormitories saw spontaneous prayer meetings take place as they did in homes across Anderson. Then people began pouring in from Kentucky, West Virginia, Illinois, Nebraska, Kansas, Canada and even California "to get a taste of the revival."

A crowd of 2000 came for a special rally on Sunday afternoon, March 8. The following Sunday afternoon, another rally drew 2,600 people, and soon, requests were coming in from pastors in many states for church members to come and tell what was happening in revival there. By the first week in May, several witness teams had gone to 31 states and Canada telling people about the Anderson revival. The pastor would say, "It wouldn't bother me at all if one Sunday morning I came to conduct the worship service and no one would be present ---as long as I knew my people were out sharing God's love with others."

As John Seamands wrote, "The revival services continued in the South Meridian Church for 50 consecutive nights (February 22 - April 12) with an average attendance of about 1,000. Barriers were broken down as members of various denominations, races and ages, all found a common meeting place at the foot of the cross. There was no fixed program and no formal preaching. A typical service lasted from two-to-three hours and consisted of singing, confession, prayer and testimony.

"Those present on one Saturday night will probably never forget the confession of a man in his mid-50s who stood before the microphone and said, 'I have been an active church member for years. I have directed many summer youth camps, but I've been a phony.'" The man also confessed how he had been hostile to people on the school board and had gone to each home and asked for forgiveness.

The Anderson revival was described as "a revival of love." One pastor said, "As God's love filled our hearts, all denominational, racial and age barriers were torn down. Congregational rifts were healed, the generation gap bridged, and families reunited." The Anderson College chaplain said, "In a day when many congregations are worried about losing their appeal to young people, Anderson's 'Revival of Love' seems to be saying something."

This revival started when seven ordinary students from Asbury College and one seminary student went to Anderson and told what God had done at Asbury. The town was turned upside down and spread across the nation. The students were only there for three days before returning to school for class. Indeed, it was as Dr. Dennis Kinlaw had observed, "The less impressive the students were, the more effective the witness was." God used a simple news release from three Asbury students to a pastor to ignite a revival that was felt for years in Anderson, Indiana and beyond.

Arthur Lindsay, in his alumni report, wrote that on Monday, March 9, "Three- thousand people crowded into the beautiful Calvary Temple in Denver, Colorado Sunday night to hear three Asbury College students, Mark Davis, Janie Wiley and David Nesselroade, share their faith in Jesus Christ. The same thing happened that had been occurring all over America for the last month.

"At the time of invitation, hundreds of people responded, stepping to the front of the sanctuary for prayer and counseling. In fact, the altar area was filled four different times. Each time the seekers were directed to a counseling room. This is typical of what has been happening in the United States since February 3, and requests for witness teams continue to pour into Asbury College from all over the nation. Invitations are now also starting to come in from foreign countries. Thus, a world-wide aspect to the revival is now beginning to take shape.

"Colombia, South America has become the second foreign country (Canada was the first) to request Asbury witness teams. Four Asburians, supported by their home churches, are in Colombia for a 10-day period of intense evangelism. So far the 1,000 students have been able to satisfy the demand, sacrificing their weekends and spring vacation. It is now estimated that more than 1,000 witness teams have gone out. Hundreds more have been sent out from Asbury Theological Seminary."

Chapter Seventeen

DAVID PERRY GOES ON A NINE-MONTH REVIVAL CRUSADE

One Asbury student who, perhaps more than any other, told the revival story dozens of times was David Perry, a ministerial student. David wrote a diary of his experiences as he covered several states from February 20 until November 17 of 1970. The Broadman Press in Nashville, Tennessee published his diary into a small book entitled *The Asbury Revival of 1970*. With his permission, thrilling reports follow of how God used him mightily over eight months, after the week of this thrilling movement of God, took place at Asbury.

As a prelude to the book, Dr. Perry pointed out that there were certain consistent characteristics in this awakening. The characteristics that were true at Asbury would spread the same to every place witness teams shared, including the churches.

NINE ASBURY REVIVAL CHARACTERISTICS

No. 1: *Spontaneous Witnessing*. "These services have been marked by numbers standing to share how Jesus Christ is making a dynamic difference in their everyday life. They are not sharing something that happened to them years ago but something up to date."

No. 2: *Confession*. "Everywhere God has walked in, He has moved people to confess things publicly, which they had been holding inside. It has been beautiful how God has kept even the confessions clean and pure. Things too unclean have not been mentioned publicly. God has impressed people to go to one another individually, when the sins have merited caution."

David Perry

No. 3: *Prayer*. "I do not recall a place that God has poured out His Spirit that has not been the result of many people praying that God would send the revival there. There was a sense of expectancy among some of the people at Asbury. Every place we have shared, people have said they had been praying that God would send a witness team to them."

No.4: *Burden*. "Those who are finding victory in their lives are no longer self-centered. They have more concern for other people now. At Asbury, students went to their friends and talked to them about a personal, up-to-date relationship with Jesus."

No. 5: *Freedom*. "In all of the services, there has been an awareness that each person is free to do what God directs him to do. People spontaneously and without instruction leave their seats to go ask forgiveness of someone. Others make public confessions. There is an obvious freedom to respond to the voice of God."

No. 6: *Laughter*. "No one has deliberately tried to be funny; however, when people stand to witness things, they have repeatedly said things that sparked spontaneous laughter. I am sure they are funny at the time because God needs to reaffirm His freedom to His people."

No. 7: *Complete Control of the Holy Spirit*. "The obvious control by God is seen, when after the story (revival account) is told, the one who is sharing sits down. No instructions are given; no invitation hymn is sung. Soon, people begin responding to that 'still small voice.' Again, we affirm this is God's revival. He will not allow an individual to take control of it or get glory from it!"

No. 8: *Love.* God's cleansing among the people has resulted in a deeper love. One person has testified that there is now a difference between being 'willing' to help someone and 'wanting' to help someone. Families have been reunited in love. A new love for the church people...the flock have found a new love for their preacher. When God walks in, love comes with Him. God is love!"

No. 9: *Continual Sharing.* "Every time God has walked in, people who have been touched by Him have gone to other places to share what they have seen. Churches ask for teams to come tell what has happened in other places. Just as hundreds of Asbury students are sharing across America, other colleges and churches are sending out witness teams also.

Chapter Eighteen

DAVID PERRY'S REVIVAL JOURNEY BEGINS WITH HIS OWN CONFESSION

David shares with transparency that during the Asbury revival, he was convicted of three big hang-ups that came out of his ego problems. He loved clothes, cars and money. As he said, "Now, I do not believe it wrong to possess these things, but my problem was that they possessed me. I told God that I wanted His plan for my life more than I wanted anything else.

"It was this commitment to Jesus that has made a difference in my motivation. I live to share Jesus with others. God has given me a love that makes me look at you, not your clothes, your car, or your money. When I walk into a crowd now, my mind is on Jesus, not myself," wrote David.

David embarked upon his eight month journey of witnessing about the Asbury revival before the week of revival was over. His diary began on February 21. "I had finished lunch with a friend, Tex Watson, when a call came from Professor Dr. Thomas Carruth to go on a witness team with him to Kingsport, Tennessee. When he said we had to leave at 1:30 p.m., I knew it was not possible for me to go. I had a Greek class at 1:00, tons of school work, and I had a date with Autumn for that night. There was no way I could contact her to break it. Tex said that he felt God wanted him to go, and as I went to class, he prepared to leave.

"As I sat down in Greek class, God began to speak to my heart, and I felt impressed to go to Kingsport. It really did not seem logical for me to go, but I asked the Lord to give me a peace if this was His will. Immediately His peace assured me of His will. I put my books in the attaché case, left a note for the professor, and walked out of the Greek class!"

"When I walked into Dr. Carruth's office, they were ready to leave. Not having time to clean up and shave, we jumped in the car and drove to Tennessee. We arrived after the service started, and again, I could not change clothes. There we were in that upper-middle class United Methodist Church. I was wearing denim jeans, an old sweater, a beard and long hair. Another guy, we discovered later, had a hole in the seat of his pants. But after we reported about the Asbury revival, God's spirit moved there among those people, and the service continued from 7:00 p.m. to 11:00 p.m.

A week later, David was asked by Dr. Carruth to go with him to the Grace United Methodist Church in Atlanta, Georgia on February 27. He began a school on prayer and asked David to share about the revival for five minutes. God moved there and they were there until March 2. Two days later, David shared the revival in a Cynthiana, Kentucky church on March 6 at a Youth in Action for Christ meeting; and then again on the next day with a team to New Columbus, Indiana near Anderson where the revival lasted for 50 consecutive days.

On March 12, David went with a team to Huntington College (IN). "Each of us testified about what God was doing in our lives, and the Spirit filled the auditorium there. When one of the professors stood and asked forgiveness of another professor, it broke loose!"

On Saturday, March 14, David's witness team arrived at Southwestern Baptist Seminary in Ft. Worth around 9 pm. They unloaded the car and went straight to a prayer meeting in the basement of the student center. "We found that the Lord had already begun this revival. We listened to confessions and prayers and witnessing just as we had experienced at Asbury. I remember looking at Parks Davis and Darius and asking, 'I wonder why we are here?'"

The next day, the team shared in seven different churches. David shared in three churches and services would run overtime by two and three hours as the Spirit moved. At Southwestern Seminary, classes are not held on Monday, but a voluntary service was called in chapel. More than 200 students and spouses were present. David and his team shared, and students confessed cheating, animosities, hatred, hostilities and bad attitudes. Students were getting right with each other. Couples were surrendering their relationships to Jesus."

David's team of three shared in three different classes on Tuesday and "God moved magnificently all day." A 3 o'clock voluntary service in Truett Auditorium continued until 6:30 as God walked in as He did in the dormitories. On Wednesday, David went to Dallas and shared at Devotion Time in the Baptist Building. "After hearing the story of the Asbury revival, everyone there went to their knees in prayer and praise to Jesus," David wrote. "From Texas I was to fly to Decatur, Illinois. I did not know where the money for the ticket would come, but I knew God would provide. I called the airport Wednesday and made the reservation. After a nearly three-hour service in Euless, Texas that night, a man asked me how and where I was going next. I told him I was flying to Decatur. He asked if I had a ticket, and then wrote out a check for the exact amount."

This was the kind of schedule that David Perry kept until late November. Everywhere he went, whether alone or with a team, he was always invited by colleges and churches to come and tell them about this exciting movement of God that took place in February at Asbury College. People were eager to hear about it, and didn't want their people to miss out on this unusual movement of God. Everywhere David went, the Holy Spirit had gone ahead and people were ready to be filled with this Spirit of Revival, and see cleansing of sin take place.

Early on after one particular service where God had moved mightily, David said, "I remember being impressed to repeatedly pray, 'Thank you and praise you, Father, Son, and Holy Spirit.'" Throughout, David had kept his word. It wasn't about him. It was about Jesus and how He wanted see people blessed and cleansed of their sins and unrighteousness. It was about people who thought they were saved but were not, but who came to an overwhelming joy when they surrendered all to Christ.

Chapter Nineteen

UNKNOWN ASBURY CALLED "HASH-BURY"..."HAS-BURY"..."ASH-BURY"

The revival was not without its humorous moments, as David explains. "Pastors would issue invitations for students to come to their churches and tell what had happened at Asbury. College leaders would issue requests also. So many times, students would just show up. They didn't know their names before they got there. Some students were even brought before crowds and their names were not mentioned as they were introduced. It didn't even matter. When they finished speaking, God began to move and revival began to break out.

"In fact, what was also interesting, was that many had never heard of Asbury. So they would call it "Hash-bury," "Has-bury," "Ash-bury" and other such names. It was really funny, but in all of this and in spite of it, God blessed powerfully everywhere students went out and told the revival story. It was glorious to experience then, and just as glorious even now, to think back on how God worked and moved in powerful ways."

On April 26, David recalls speaking at the First Nazarene Church in Ada, Oklahoma at 6 p.m. "I began sharing at 6:00 and at 6:30 I had them bow their heads. Without any warning, God prompted me to leave the pulpit and walk out of the church. Later they told us that God walked into that service and people started going to the altar, praying, witnessing and confessing. It lasted until 9:00.

"At 7:00 p.m. I was in the First Baptist Church there. It was a full house, and God's presence was sensed before the service began. The revival broke out here and lasted until 9:30." Obeying the Spirit had become an important characteristic of David's amazing ministry, seeking no praise but that Jesus Christ would be glorified for His profound Presence that led to such an awakening.

David did take time on September 18, 1970, as he and Autumn Gayl Creeks were married. They had met at Asbury College prior to the great revival. Both were transformed. Autumn had also been on witness teams. After their wedding, God provided them with a Winnebago Motor Home, and they continued sharing the Asbury revival together in colleges, churches and places where invited. God moved everywhere they went.

David, Autumn, and the Winnebago

Fast forward almost 50 years and I found that David and Autumn were living in Milledgeville, Georgia, just 30 miles from where David grew up in Gordon. David had pastored churches since his seminary days at Asbury Seminary. He came out of retirement to take a small Baptist church outside of Milledgeville and today to no one's surprise, it is on fire for God.

David speaks with great joy and emotion as he recalls those Asbury revival days and the months that followed where he went to states to tell the story and revival broke out. "I remember that Dr. Jack Gray of Southwestern Baptist Seminary would go with us to places in Texas. One of the things I remember him saying was the hardest thing was to have patience and let the Holy Spirit work and not the pastor. We would share what God had done at Asbury and in other places since the revival. We would not give an invitation, we asked the musicians not to play or sing, and we would simply sit down on the front row and wait.

"You know pastors are trained to be in charge. Sometimes it would be instant when someone shared and other times, maybe five minutes, but that would seem like an eternity of silence. And then, just like at Asbury, someone would be led to walk up to the front and kneel down. Or, they may stand and confess sins or profess Christ as Savior. And then it was like a release of the Holy Spirit every time that would happen. Then I would go to the platform and really direct traffic as people sought to confess sins publicly. Some wanted to share, some wanted to invite Christ into their heart, while some wanted to be prayed for and give Jesus lordship over their life.

"Then some would immediately have a burden for unsaved friends. They would leave and bring them into the service, and so many were saved that way.

"All those services were much alike but not one the same. It was like Dr. (Dennis) Kinlaw had said, "It was just like God walked in. We know he is omni-present but I learned during the revival that there are three levels of His presence. First, there is His omnipresence. You cannot escape Him and you may not know Him.

"Second, there is the unconscious presence. The Psalmist said, "God, why did you leave me?" Well, He didn't. We can have sin in our lives and may not be aware of His presence.

"But third, revival is the manifest presence of God. In His presence, He is the fullness of joy. He can first come as conviction because I'm not right with God as a believer. But in His presence, it is manifested. Just like when you walked into Hughes Auditorium for the first time in your own experience there."

When the Asbury revival came, David was a first-year Asbury Seminary student. He had graduated from Asbury College in 1969 and his wife-to-be, Autumn, was a senior at Asbury and would graduate with the class of 1970. "It only took less than a couple of days for the revival to break out across the street at the seminary," David said. "I went to her dorm and got her, and we walked into Hughes Auditorium together. Sometimes we would go eat separately and then together. But in it all, God was convicting me of my pride and selfish ambition, and my quest for clothes, cars and money.

"E. Stanley Jones' book on *Victory Through Surrender* helped convict me. I went to a telephone and called my parents. My Dad was a Methodist pastor and I confessed some things to them and asked for their forgiveness. Missionary students were calling their parents overseas. Pretty soon, people all over the country and overseas were calling in and saying, 'Whoa, what is God doing? I want to be there.' Within two or three days, people would literally walk into the foyer and take their shoes off before entering. Not everybody did it, but when they did, everybody knew why they were doing it. God was there. It was a natural response, like Moses when he took his shoes off in the presence of God."

Immediately, David became submissive to God, and it came with his car, a 1967 Chevrolet Chevelle Super Sport that he dearly loved. "I loved cars and I had a sports car. When the invitations came in to send students to their places, I started traveling. So many times, I would fly to places and one day Dr. Carruth had students who needed a car to go out and witness. He said, 'David, you have a car. So, I gave him the keys in his office and said to him, 'Well, it's not my car. It's God's. So, students used that car and wore it out. I don't know how many miles they put on it going all over and sharing the story of the Asbury revival.

"For me, I didn't want to part with it. I didn't want them to scratch it. But, I literally gave it away to God at that altar. For me, it was absolute assurance that God had delivered me from that envy, pride and selfishness. But God used that car, which I thought was mine, until I gave it away. God used it for His Glory until the end of the year."

Chapter Twenty
THE ASBURY REVIVAL FLAME HAS NEVER GONE OUT

For a revival movement of this magnitude, it didn't end that year of 1970. The revival flame implanted in the hearts and souls of many students never went out. The fire was always there. The experience was such that the fire never left them. Gary Wright was a student who was on the witness team to South Meridian Church of God in Anderson, Indiana. He would say later, "Some say as many as 5,000-7,000 made commitments to Christ during the 50 days of nightly services, which outgrew church facilities and moved into the civic auditorium." Revival swept the church, Anderson University and the city.

Twenty-one years later, Gary was to bring the last message at "Spiritual Emphasis Week" at Bethel College in Mishawaka, Indiana. In his words Gary says, "I was sitting on the front row of Bethel Chapel and was given only 20 minutes to speak. I had a problem. I sensed God was asking me to share about the 1970 Asbury/Anderson revival, including my testimony of being filled with the Holy Spirit. How could I do that in 20 minutes? I prayed, 'Lord, you know me. I cannot say 'Hello' in 20 minutes; this seems impossible.

"As I sat on that front row next to my dear friends, Bob and Marilyn Ham, I had an old spiritual sensation inside. It took me back 21 years to the Anderson revival. I felt heaviness in my chest that I remembered feeling as I walked up the steps to the pulpit on Saturday evening that first day of the Anderson revival. It is hard to explain that feeling. I regard it as spiritual, yet it feels physical. It is the weight of His glory.

"In Scripture, 'God's Glory' is defined as that which has weight (Note: The Hebrew word 'glory' is derived from the root 'heavy') as with gold or silver. One feels the physical weight of His presence. His glory contains His Holiness. One can at times sense one's own lack of 'holy' and that of others. God seems to have at times allowed me to sense the burden of sin in people's lives. At its strongest it seems at times to take my breath away. I thought to myself as I waited to preach, 'God is going to do it again.' In the next 20 minutes, He did it again.

"People started walking to the altar of chapel that day, before I could finish. Maybe as many as 50 to 70 people knelt, and prayed and wept. Soon people were apologizing to each other over one of the microphones. I thought to myself, 'This looks and feels real.'

"It truly has proven to be real revival. I remember sensing the Lord speak to me, saying, 'Your work is finished, do not say another word.' I saw an empty seat that someone had vacated on the back row of the chapel so, without saying another word, I walked off the pulpit area and sat in that seat. Again, I sensed the Lord speaking to me, 'He said, you are done, leave now!' I got up and went to one of the campus leaders and explained that I needed to be on my way. I went to the room where I was staying, packed my bags, and left. I did not return until two years later when we visited the campus."

When Gary told this story in 2016 to Robert Kanary in his book, *Spontaneous Revivals*, he summarized the long-term results of that 1991 service with the students. "When the students and faculty left Bethel that weekend, the revival went with them. It spread quickly through the entire Missionary Church denomination. According to then Missionary Church, President Dr. John Moran, the revival had an enduring effect on the denomination that has lasted to this day. Bethel College certainly has never been the same. It has tripled in size as students who seek a deeper relationship with Christ have recognized the spiritual depth on campus. Chapel services continue to be a place where people can experience God."

You can trace this movement of God at Bethel College in 1991 all the way back to 1967, when Jeannine Brabon began to pray for revival; when she gathered other Asbury students to pray, leading to the week of revival there on February 3-10 in 1970. The work of God goes beyond our wildest imagination on how He uses people. In this case, he used college students, to expand the Kingdom of God as he did through Gary Wright at Bethel, a college in Indiana, that lives on today.

Chapter Twenty-One

50 YEARS LATER: FEBRUARY 2-3, 2020 SUNDAY AFTERNOON HUGHES AUDITORIUM

Some 300 Asbury graduates and friends gathered in Hughes Auditorium on Sunday afternoon at 4 p.m. to begin a two-day celebration of the 1970 Revival that took place 50 years before. How special it was to sit in the same seats that students sat in at chapel on that historic morning when revival came to Asbury College. This was one anniversary that commanded celebrating and rejoicing in the Lord. Asbury leaders made it special.

Dean Stu Smith presided and welcomed everyone who came from across America and many countries throughout the world. The afternoon session began with two thrilling songs of the faith. The first was "Jesus, What a Friend of Sinners…Hallelujah, What a Friend" they sang, "Saving, helping, keeping, loving, He is with me 'til the end." Then they sang out to "Holiness, Holiness, Holiness is what I long for."

Stu said that he was a 1977 Asbury graduate and had spent 32 years serving at the college. Twenty of those years he had served as Dean and Campus Chaplain. He gave a short testimony of his 1970 revival experience. "I was 15 years old. My dad was on the faculty and my mother was a staff member. I spent most of my time in the gym playing basketball or in the cafeteria. When the revival started, I slipped into the back of Hughes Auditorium. I sensed God's presence and held onto the back wall to keep from going forward. I took it all in as I heard one testimony after another. I saw students who were not that close to God tell of what the Lord had done in their lives. It was so real and genuine.

"Mother played the piano for many of the songs. I'd see reporters come in and sit for what I thought would be for 30 minutes, and they'd sit for two or three hours. I came all week as I saw God was for real. His presence was unmistaken. Yet, without committing myself, it was a pivotal point in my life.

"Then in the gym one day in 1973, I came to total surrender of my life to Jesus Christ. I made my way over to Hughes Auditorium, came to the center of this altar and sealed my surrender where the Holy One had come three years before. Over the past 50 years, I have prayed with students at this altar many times. This place is special because the Holy One is here."

After Stu's thrilling story, he introduced the special 1970 documentary film, *When God Comes*, highlighting the events of the 1970 revival. It was produced in 1995, and the film was introduced by Henry Blackaby, international speaker and author of *Experiencing God*. No doubt, most everyone present had seen the film many times but never resist seeing it again. How thrilling to see actual footage of the revival that shook the Asbury campus when Jesus visited in power and glory.

After watching the documentary, there was a short break. Then, Jeannie Banter, Assistant Director of Spiritual Life on campus, came to the podium and welcomed the alumni, friends, faculty and staff. In her prayer, she thanked God for what He had done, is doing and what is yet to come. She said, "God is on the move still here at Asbury. Last week, we had Holiness Emphasis Week and students came to this altar seeking God. The Cross behind me is filled with confessions of sin of those who want to walk in freedom."

Then Jeannie read thrilling words of testimony that included students from 1970, and in last week's Holiness Emphasis Week.

"Christ met me and I'm different…Last night the Holy Spirit flooded in and filled my life…This week, God helped me to stand back up…There are tears, release, freedom, repentance and joy unspeakable…God empowered me to the Holy Spirit to speak truth in love without fear.

"I sat in Hughes last night and just let Jesus love me…God reminded me of the importance of intimacy with Him…God moved in my life by beginning the sanctification process and giving me a strong support of other believers to continue in the next steps. Praise the Lord."

Chapter Twenty-Two

BETH KINLAW COPPEDGE IMPARTS MOVING REVIVAL MOMENTS

Jeannie then introduced Beth Coppedge, a 1969 Asbury graduate who was Beth Kinlaw at that time, since President Dennis Kinlaw was her father. Beth and her husband, Al, went from Asbury to Costa Rica, then Colombia as missionaries for four years. She founded *Titus Women*, and has led women in personal holiness and discipleship for all these years. Dr. Coppedge was a former professor at the Asbury Theological Seminary and together they teach in conferences and seminars across America and beyond today.

Everyone in Hughes Auditorium was excited to hear what Beth had to say. After the singing of *Blessed Assurance* and *There's a Sweet, Sweet Spirit In This Place*, Beth read from Exodus 17:8-15, the story of Moses' victory over Amalek and the altar he built and called it, 'The Lord is my banner.' Then she began to tell her revival memories. "I remember one day when I was in high school, Mother said to me one morning, 'Bethy, could you ever stay home from school with me today?' Oh, I assured her that I could. I said, 'What did you have in mind, Mom?' She was a great little woman of prayer.

"She said, 'Well Honey, I have such a burden for revival in Wilmore and in the Asbury institutions, and I just need somebody to kneel with me.' So I found myself as an 17-year old kneeling beside my Mother all day long by the side of her bed. She prayed through Psalm 20 and she claimed it. She was so cute as she prayed for the Lord to answer in the day of trouble. She said, 'Lord, we are in trouble' and she prayed in the name of the God of Jacob. She said Israel instead of Jacob, because she felt it gives more hope. And then she said, 'May you send help from your sanctuary to our college, our town, our community and our nation. We need help. Would you strengthen us out of Zion?'

Beth Kinlaw Coppedge speaking

"And then she said, 'Would you remember our offerings, our burnt sacrifices, our worship? And Lord would you grant according to My heart's desire what is your heart's desire? Oh Jesus, would you come and fulfill your heart's desire for our institutions, our college, our seminary and our town? Would you fulfill your purposes so that we can rejoice in your salvation and in the name of God, we can set up our banners? Would you fulfill the prayers in our hearts that You are praying for us, dear Holy Spirit, dear Lord Jesus Christ?'

"As I sat and knelt there, I knew I was on Holy Ground. There began to be in me a hunger to know God, not just about Him but to know Him face to face and nose to nose. And verse six of Psalm 20 says 'now I know,' and it's that Hebrew word *yada,*' that intimate knowledge that the Lord saves His anointed. He answers from His holy Heaven, with the saving strength of his right hand. Some trust in chariots and some in horses, but we trust in the name of the Lord our God.

"Nothing happened at that time, but it didn't deter her and she continued to pray with five or six women each Thursday to ask Jesus to come to Wilmore for revival. I remember in 1970, when revival came, Al and I were already married and were in language school in Costa Rica. My sister sent me a card and she wrote, 'Guess what Jesus sent Mama for her birthday? A revival.' It wasn't a surprise to any one of her five children. We all just thought, well that fits. And then, Mother sent us a cassette tape and Al took it to the Chapel. There were 80 of us missionaries in language school that would eventually spread all over Latin America after we had been there a year.

"As we listened so eagerly, and before Lynn Smith had even finished playing *There's a Sweet, Sweet Spirit In This Place*, we as a corporate body were on our faces before the Holy God. The beautiful thing about that was, that when the year was over, we were all over Latin America with that revival spirit in our hearts. Every single one of us could attest that we had a personal encounter with the Holy One, even through a cassette player. He came to Papa in a phone booth in Alaska. He came to us through an old cassette recorder in Costa Rica. God came. And I want to say to you today, it has been 50 years ago, but God is still in the redemptive business. And I want to know today, on whom are you relying, not then but now? In whom do you trust? Some trust in horses, some in chariots, but they will bow down and fall, but some trust in God.

"My prayer is as we meet on this 50th anniversary at Asbury in Hughes Auditorium, once again, the Shekinah Glory would move in our souls and we would never, ever be the same again. And those of us who have gray hairs would begin to intercede until Jesus can be raised up in the generations yet to come, so the generations yet to come can say that God met my mother, my grandmother, my father, my uncle, my neighbor lady, my pastor's wife. I know it because God met them in my life over 50 years ago for revival.

"Oh Holy Jesus, would you come now? There's a sweet, sweet spirit in this place. We invite you not as our guest, but as our host. We worship you for what you have done before and we remember. Lord

Jesus, would you come again? You always come when you are invited. In the name of the Father, in the name of the Son and in the name of the Holy Spirit of God."

How appropriate that Dr. Dennis Kinlaw's daughter, Beth, such a godly and sweet saint of the Spirit, was there to give such a moving message 50 years later in the same room where the revival took place. Her mother, the Asbury president's wife, had begun to pray earnestly with Beth five years before the revival came. Beth would not have dreamed that she would be on the mission field when her Mother's prayers were answered, and it was far beyond their wildest comprehension when it came.

Chapter Twenty-Three

STEVE SEAMANDS SPEAKS OF WHAT HE SAW AND HEARD

Following Beth was Dr. Steve Seamands, who was an Asbury senior when the Revival came. Dr Seamands is now Professor Emeritus at Asbury Theological Seminary. He began with one of his favorite descriptions of revival by Jonathan Edwards during the First Great Awakening. He wrote, "Revival is the acceleration and intensification of the normal work of the Holy Spirit. It seems as if that during revival, God can take what might happen in 1,000 years and make it happen in a day." Steve said, "Those of us who were here in 1970 certainly experienced the acceleration and intensification of the normal working of the Holy Spirit.

"This was not a revival that was rooted in preaching or teaching. It was rooted in confession and conviction of sin. It led to answered prayers and testimonies. I remembered praying with Tim Philpot and seeing him born again right before my eyes here at this altar. It was physically intense during those days at the altar. A spirit of obedience sort of took over. It was wonderful to watch.

"I had lived in Wilmore the previous five years, and those were turbulent years in this little village. There was a class before me that had four different college presidents. There was a lot of conflict and misunderstanding. There were people who had hurt people and were not speaking to each other. I remember seeing two men who were at odds with each other that had divided the community, putting their arms around each other in the back of the auditorium in forgiveness.

"And then when obedience comes to you, there will be power given to you in your witness. Three weeks after the revival, Carol and I went to visit her parents in Ohio, and Debbie Fulton went with us. Her brother in Warren, Ohio heard that we were up there and he called on Saturday and said the pastor would like for you to share the revival in church tomorrow morning. Reluctantly, we said yes. Debbie went first and shared what was going on in her life with the 150 or so people present.

"I got up and told the story of how the revival started and unfolded. I was about five to seven minutes into my story, and suddenly a woman on the back row stood up and just blurted out. She started talking to the pastor and confessing how she had spoken about him harshly, criticized him and said some ugly things about him. People just started running to the altar. I remember Carol's brother running and sobbing as he ran to the altar.

"I remember watching this whole thing, and I didn't even get to give an invitation (huge laughter from the audience). Later on, I thought to myself, I think I could have just gotten up there and said, 'Mary had a little lamb, its fleece was white as snow', and people would have come. The power of the Holy Spirit is accelerated and intensified in seasons of revival."

Dr. Seamands then said that many times he has been asked, what was the greatest impact of the revival on you? "It wasn't about memories of the past, but what it did for my imagination. It gave me longings and expectations of what God could do in the future. I had seen it happen. It sort of amped up what I consider to be the normal work of the Holy Spirit. It caused me to think, Lord, I've seen that. I want to see that again. I want to see that again. It shaped the way I prayed. The Asbury revival of the past should cause us to pray with expectancy for what God wants to do even now.

"I ran across these words from Andrew Murray earlier today, "Beware in your prayers above all else of limiting God, not only by unbelief, but fantasizing you know what He can do. Expect unexpected things above all that we could ask or think." Thank God for that revival and what it can do for us as we pray, not limiting God, but we have seen what He can do. So we say, O God, come and do it again as it says in Psalm 85. Lord won't you revive us again so that your people will rejoice in you. Come Lord Jesus. Come Holy Spirit."

Chapter Twenty-Four

FORMER PRESIDENT SANDRA GRAY AND PRESIDENT KEVIN BROWN CLOSE OUT THE AFTERNOON SESSION

After Beth and Dr. Seamands delivered such heart rending accounts of their revival experience, President Kevin Brown rose to greet the people who had gathered from near and far for this anniversary celebration. Dr. Brown became the 18th President of Asbury University in the summer of 2019.

His remarks began with the importance of 'remembering,' as pointed out time and time again in the Scriptures. God said, "Remember the former things of old" in Isaiah 46." He cited other Scriptures and said, "These things speak to the past to remember what has been, but in the universe of Christianity in the Kingdom of God, we possess a unique understanding and application of memory. In Scripture, memory is not bound to the past. It is just as much a vision of what is to be. This is why you hear theologians say, 'remember the future.' It doesn't make a lot of sense, but if we have a Kingdom mentality, it does. Remember the future.

"So today, as we gather to celebrate God's spirit, we remember the revival of 1970. But in that celebration, with equal jubilance, excitement, participation and awe, let us celebrate God's reviving and renewing spirit that is here in our presence now. May our active participation, our collective memory of the past, presence and future be an ever continuing manifold witness of God's reviving, renewing, his saving and his sanctifying victory in the lives of His people.

"I stand before you today not simply appreciative, not simply sentimental, though I am both. I stand before you today expectant. Remember the past, let us remember the future.

"And now, it's my deep honor to introduce Dr. Sandra Gray, who was the first President of Asbury University (the college became a university in 2010). We continue to harvest the fruitful abundance of the great work she has done in the past here. She loves the Lord and I am deeply honored to call her friend."

Dr. Gray, who had served 12 years as Asbury president, addressed the audience saying "This will be a time of directed prayer, and we are going to begin with confession. Revival really begins with us. I want us to spend some time with our own confession and repentance, acknowledging our personal needs and for some of us, sometimes that's uncomfortable. I'm going to call us to get quiet, and it's going to be private prayer, personal prayer and call for a deep hush to settle in over Hughes Auditorium as we look into the Holy Spirit. The Holy Spirit is within us and ask Him to reveal the things in me, the things in you that stand as a hindrance to the Holy Spirit in what he wants to do in our own deep needs."

Then she asked the audience to spend private time in prayer for several minutes. What a place Hughes Auditorium is to be silent. Reflex in such a place, where the presence of Jesus is so strongly felt, and call upon Him in confession and repentance. It feels like an honor to sit and pray in such a hallowed and holy place of God in prayer.

Then she read II Chronicles 7:14, the great revival verse, and led the crowd to enter into a time of intercession. She invited this time to be a time of intercession, corporate prayer for the church, for God's people, for the lost. She invited anyone to prayer, as two people would pass microphones for those led to pray. And pray they did, heartfelt prayers by several to transform us again, to move upon our hearts, to come in your fullness, to recognize that His power is within us. One prayer was a plea for renewal of the church, to see us restored in faith and obedience, and that our nation would return to Him.

Others prayed that we have more of You, O God, and that the Glory of the Lord would cover the earth as the waters cover the sea. Create in us a clean heart and create a right spirit within us, restore the joy of our salvation, and do it again Lord, do it again.

Then Dr Gray read from Habakkuk 3:18-19, "We will rejoice in the Lord. The sovereign Lord is our strength and He makes us as sure footed as the deer, and able to tread upon the heights." Then she asked the crowd to stand and lift up praises together unto the Lord and offer up prayers of praise and thanksgiving, and let the Lord hear a mighty chorus of praise. People raised up praises to God all over the auditorium and this afternoon of great celebration closed with the singing of *Great Is Thy Faithfulness* to the joy of every heart.

Chapter Twenty-Five

THE 50TH ANNIVERSARY CHAPEL SERVICE IN HUGHES AUDITORIUM

The 50th anniversary of the Asbury College 1970 Revival came on a beautiful day in Wilmore on Monday, February 3, 2020. It was so unlike the snow that covered the campus 50 years ago. Today, it was sunny and 65 degrees. For years, this day had been anticipated by Asbury University, the Wilmore community, alums who experienced the Revival and friends from across America and from many mission fields scattered throughout the world. Asbury has only 22,000 alumni but is among the highest Christian colleges in America in sending foreign missionaries to serve the world.

For me as a student of revival history, the honor of being in Hughes Auditorium on this very special day was a bit overwhelming. As one who appreciates revival history, and recognizing the significance of this revival in American history, it was an ethereal moment, too perfect to experience. Barbara and I arrived at 9:30 a.m. as alumni were delirious with joy and excitement, greeting friends, enjoying the moment and choosing their seats. Typical with students for chapel, most did not arrive until 9:50 a.m. but they were in their assigned seats by 10 a.m. How thrilling to sit in chapel again, as I did in my college days at Howard College, now Samford University.

Also accompanying us, from the Billy Graham Evangelistic Association in Charlotte, were Emily Adams and Raquel Arbogast, who have a heart cry for revival and rejoiced in their first visit to Asbury.

After the Sunday evening service, students placed yellow sheets on the back of seats that would be available to alumni and friends like us. Some were single seats and others found seats together. They were scattered empty seats all over the room. What a blessing to be seated with the bright Asbury students. Hughes Auditorium of 1,500 seats was filled. Your mind began to race back 50 years to this moment when chapel began that day and Jesus walked in. You felt His very presence just walking in, seeing the people mixing, taking seats and then watching those students rush in and speaking to those seated next to you. It was good finding out who they were, where they were from and what they were studying.

Barbara and I chose two seats three-quarters of the way back in the center aisle. I wanted to observe the students most of all and catch a good view of every angle of the auditorium for this service. The organist was playing a hymn as the alums, students, faculty and friends gathered. Then Greg Haseloff, the Asbury Campus Chaplain, stepped to the podium at 10 a.m.

"This is a very special day," said Greg, "as we welcome Asburians young and old and those who are listening to this service around the world, including friends in India who are praying for revival in our country and holding us up in prayer this morning. As we look back to 1970, videos and stories have told us that God came here. It was one divine moment, and today we celebrate with stories of lives that were transformed. We gather not to worship revival, but to worship the One who has given himself to us; the One who is present with us this morning, and we worship the One who invites us to himself."

Greg pointed out, "Many revivals have marked Asbury's history from the first two decades; then in the 1930's; a significant move of God in 1950; in 1958; in 1992; and the 1970 revival made an impact on dozens of campuses and hundreds of churches. Through the media, many stories were captured, and today we are going to hear many of them on how God worked."

Then the Asbury Chapel Praise Team led in singing, "Praise forever to the King of Kings. I've seen you move the mountains and I believe I see you do it again." The audience stood for a time of praise and worship. How thrilling to observe students who raised their hands in worship, jump up and down, spun themselves around unashamedly as they expressed their adoration to Jesus. You sensed that there are Asbury students praying and have a hunger for revival again on this campus. They were aware of the mighty moves of God on this campus and wanted Him to do it again.

The praise singing was followed by President Kevin Brown who said, "Fifty years ago today, students gathered for a regular chapel. But a chapel that would end 185 hours later. Today, you will hear the extraordinary story of the 1970 revival, a movement of God's spirit that forever marked the lives of those who experienced it. It was a movement that forever changed Asbury College and now Asbury University.

"To our students and to our guests, this morning I want to ask you, 'What is your revival story?' The 1970 revival inspires reflection, appreciation, celebration, and remembrance. I want to remind you that it would be a mistake to relocate these sentiments to some bygone era. Asbury is many things, but we are not a museum. The revival is not simply a spiritual heirloom of faithful men and women who have gone before us. It is a real living presence, and an active thing, because we serve a real, living, present and active God."

He went on to share a personal story about a day soon after he came to Asbury, seven years ago when he joined the staff. A personal time of prayer alone in Hughes Auditorium came to a time of complete surrender to God. "I gave in, and in that moment, God met me. I was different. In that moment, I found a strength and a power and a fullness that I live into today. This is the great irony of Christianity, in that emptying ourselves, we become whole.

"So Asbury students, what is your revival story? Revival is living, active and present, but it is also spiritual oxygen. Revival is power. It is our power to live in the words of St. Paul; to live upright, godly lives in this present age. It is the power to become less, so that someone else can become more. That power lasts forever. His power, His kingship, His rulership is forever in reign. What is your revival story, this morning?"

Alums heard from their recently installed president, Dr. Brown, and what a heart for prayer and revival he has. The university leader is a man of God and has a revival heart himself.

Chapter Twenty-Six
STAN KEY PAINTS A POWERFUL PICTURE OF REVIVAL

Following Dr. Brown to the platform was Rev. Stan Key, President of the Francis Asbury Society, a former missionary and pastor, and a 1975 Asbury graduate.

Rev. Key gave a stirring message entitled "What Is Revival" from Ezekiel 37, which he called "the classic statement of revival in all of Scripture." It is the great story of the revival of the dry bones. He read beginning with the first verse, "The hand of the Lord came upon me and brought me out in the Spirit of the Lord, and set me down in the midst of the valley, and it was full of bones." Rev. Key read the passage through verse 14, on how God brought the dry bones back to life as a great army, and they knew that the Lord had performed it.

His message had three points on, "What it looks like when God comes." He began in this way. "I want to suggest that there are three ingredients to a revival from Heaven. The first is a 'Vision of the Valley.' Somebody has got to see the truth about the condition of the people of God and the church. God said to Ezekiel, what do you see? And he said, 'Lord, I see a cemetery.' Genuine and authentic revival always begins with conviction of sin and an awareness of our spiritual death. It's what Jesus said to the church at Sardis, I know your works. You have the reputation of being alive, but you are dead, dead as a doornail. That's when revival comes.

"I came on the campus of Asbury three years after the revival, trying to make sense out of this strange place. One of the revival speakers for the fall revival here was Leonard Ravenhill. Some called him Leonard "Ravenmad" because he stood in this pulpit and basically scared the hell out of me. And I did not swear when I said that. And I realized that was what he was intending to do, scare the hell out of us. He told me that I was a sinner, a hypocrite and if I didn't change I would go to hell. Prophets are never very popular people. But, oh, the freedom that comes when you get to a place where you realize that I'm just a no good, low-down dirty rotten bum, and everybody else is to and they know I am. Isn't it a glorious reality to live in?

"Revival came to this campus 50 years ago when some students were praying. Jeannine Brabon is going to tell you later this morning when she walked around this campus with a ring of cards praying the names of students who needed God in their life. Rumor has it that she was rather obnoxious on campus, because people don't like to be reminded of the spiritual death. But that's when God comes because, where sin abounds, grace abounds even more. It's when we empty ourselves that we discover the fullness of God, and that's what happened in this room 50 years ago…the glorious reality."

Rev. Key's second point was the "Proclamation of the Word." He referenced how Ezekiel proclaimed the Word to the dry bones and Jesus proclaimed the Word to Lazarus and he came forth. They were delivered from darkness and death by the Word. "What I understand about the 1970 revival is that the Word of God came into this room, not primarily through preaching, as important as that is. The Word came through testimony. But it was the Word as students and faculty stood at the microphone in obedience to the Word of God.

"Those are two good and important points, but that's not revival until, thirdly, 'the Breath of the Spirit' is applied. Ezekiel had to preach to the bones and to the wind. God told him to breathe across this valley. The bones began to come together, formed corpses and the Spirit of God said preach to the breath. And this is when it happened, the sweet, sweet breath of the Almighty breathed into those cadavers and they began to come awake. They stood on their feet, a mighty army, and I think they turned to the Lord their God and they said, 'Sir, reporting for duty.' That's a great story.

"We celebrate something that happened 50 years ago, not because we are interested in nostalgia or sentimentality. We celebrate the past to remind us that God wants to do it again. I think my favorite statement on revival comes from G. Campbell Morgan who said years ago, 'We can't create revival, but we can set our sails for the wind of the Spirit when it begins to blow.'

"One of my daughters reminded me of Prince Caspian by C.S. Lewis, where Lucy is talking to Aslan and saying, 'You came but you didn't come the same way you came last time.' And Aslan says to Lucy, 'Things never happen the same way twice.' They happen, but let God have the freedom. Lord Jesus, that you would rend the Heavens and come down, that you would manifest Your presence to us with the essential ingredients that let us know it is really You. It's not just emotions, it's not just hype, it's the sanctifying Spirit bringing life. In the name of Jesus and the hope of the kingdom, Amen.

Rev. Key's message in olden days would have made the Methodists shout. It was magnificent in reminding the alumni and friends of a true Biblical revival, and clearly presenting to the students a clear message of revival. His message was followed by showing again the 25-minute film, "*When God Comes*," the story of the Asbury 1970 revival with actual footage of that blessed week. It was produced in 1995.

The film was introduced by Dr. Henry Blackaby, an international evangelical pastor, preacher and author. He said, "Many of us today are spending a portion of every prayer time asking God to send upon us a spirit of prayer, supplication, and revival. There is something within us that continues to yearn for God in a personal and an intimate way and revival is such a very important part of that process. Revival, though, is rather unpredictable because God does that in His own time and in His own way. And we never know when or how we will experience that mighty movement of God as He moves among us in revival.

"I see indications of a searching and longing for revival today. I see it on college campuses, churches, and in many other kinds of schools across the United States and Canada. As a matter of fact, across our world. But few examples, past or present, show the presence and power of the Holy Spirit, and worked so clearly with such an impact, and the remarkable events that accompanied that, which took place at Asbury College in the town of Wilmore, Kentucky in February of 1970. And as you will see, that light and the presence and power of God is moving again in a mighty way across our land."

Chapter Twenty-Seven
JEANNINE BRABON MESSAGE 50 YEARS LATER

After the 1970 Revival was told in the documentary, "When God Comes," the packed Hughes Auditorium was ready with great anticipation to hear from Jeannine Brabon, who was the prayer leader for this historic campus revival that spread across America and parts of the world. She came to the anniversary from Colombia, South America where she has serves as a missionary since her Asbury college days. Winning 1,367 souls to Christ individually in 2019, shows that this woman and saint of God is a true walking revival. Her walk with the Lord has been exemplary of a true revival leader.

Jeannine started with a prayer, which was most appropriate for her, one who has lived a life of prayer. "Lord Jesus, I just pray right now that You will enable me to tell Your story, my own story, Lord, of revival. Come. Thank You, Jesus, in Your precious name, Amen." Then she looked over Hughes Auditorium and began. "One of the things that I saw

Jeannine with the author and his wife, Barbara

early on is that obedience is the key to revival. God loves to do the impossible through the most unlikely. How would you respond if you knew your obedience to God would have a significant impact for all of eternity?

"In Genesis 12, we are told of Abraham's call and Abraham responded and departed as the Lord told him. Like Abraham, my father left all in obedience and went as a missionary to South America where I was born. I have a very rich heritage. At age 5, I accepted Jesus as my Lord and Savior. I grew up in the Interamerican church in Colombia. We had a very difficult time, but in the community, I noticed a difference. At age 10, I went to my Mother and I said, "Mother, how come adults never get angry?' She said two words. 'Jeannine, it is the Holy Spirit.' Well, I knew that I needed it in my life.

"When I was 11, I never fit into the North American culture. I never felt like I belonged. During the summer at a missionary convention at the end of a message by Bill Gillam, I felt God was calling me to serve Him. I remember going home that night and cried myself to sleep. I didn't feel I had what it would take. I didn't feel that I had it all together. To be a missionary in my context, I knew that you had to lay down your life. I remember seminary students coming from ministry with their heads split open by machetes. I remember people who were martyred for their faith. I felt, 'How God can You possibly use me?' but availability is what God wants. Still, I had a hunger in my heart for the Lord Jesus.

"When I was age 12, I got home from a meeting in our church in Medellin, I knelt down by my bed, and I just poured out my heart to God. I was honest with Him. I said, 'Lord, I don't like to read the Bible. I know I should read the Bible. I know I should witness but I am scared to death to witness.' I'd walk outside our campus and we'd get rocks thrown at us because they hated Protestants. I said, I don't have a lot of courage, Lord. I told the Lord just how I felt and I sensed the Lord come upon me in a new way. That morning, I woke up, grabbed my Bible, started reading my Bible, and had a hunger for it.

"I went to school. We were a one-room school that we used from primary to junior high. We went out to play a game. I got a foul called on me and I didn't react like I normally reacted. No anger. I said that's okay. I was dumbfounded. What happened to me? So I went to my teacher, John Putney, a Wesleyan missionary, and told him what happened. He said, 'Jeannine, it's the Holy Spirit." I said, Holy Spirit, you just take me. That's the only way I want to live. I found a purity and a passion not of my own and I wanted to know God intimately. I felt very insignificant, but I came to know the One who is significant…God Almighty. I didn't feel worthy or capable. This is the very condition that God wanted. Obedience is where God has brought me today.

"In working in the prisons today in Colombia, I cling to one thing I learned as a teenager. Security is not having it altogether. Security is the presence of Jesus. It's all about relationship. Why did Jesus pray? It was his relationship with the Father. I began to live in revival. What do you mean by that? Well, the song says, 'Oh, for a heart to praise my God. A heart from sin set free, A heart that fully feels the blood so free shed for me.'

"I realized that I wanted God to work in a deeper way. He began to work in my life and He had called me into prayer. 'How can I do something more?' and the Lord said, 'I want you to pray every hour.' 'So how can I pray every hour?' The Lord said, 'You pray before class,' so I began to pray for people every hour in an earnest way, even five years before the revival ever began here. It was a difficult time when I came to Asbury. There were riots in our country, Vietnam, there was turmoil on our campus. When I was a freshman, students came up to me with a petition to get the president out. The Lord just said to me, Jeannine, you can criticize or you can pray. To criticize is talking to men. To pray, you are talking to Me. So, God called me to pray for a move of God that would impact the world beginning here on our campus.

"I was just a freshman, but I never missed chapel. It wasn't always that exciting, but I was waiting for God to come. My sophomore year, the Lord challenged me to pray before chapel. I was very shy and felt very insignificant. I went to the spiritual life coordinator, and she sent me to the student body president. I felt, O Lord, how many more people do I have to talk to for a room to pray. He sent me to the academic dean. He said, what do you want? I said, I feel within my spirit that we need a room to pray before chapel and he said go find one. I found a place to pray and I wanted a lot of students to pray but there wasn't that many of us.

"But there was a pocket of students who began to pray, who had a hunger to see God work in a special way. I can remember my junior year, the Lord said, 'Jeannine, I want you to pray for every student in the student body.' So I went to the registrar's office and I said, 'I want to pray for every student by name. Every student is precious to Jesus and I want to lift them to Jesus. Would it be possible to get a list of the student body?' and I got a list! I put it in a binder and I carried it everywhere with me, and I prayed over every single student, praying that Jesus would touch their lives and come.

"My class was the Aztecs, and in October of 1969 in the *Aztec Action*, I wrote, 'Many sincere Christians are aware of the need for revival. There is a deep need for the Holy Spirit to take action in a greater way, whether it be our home communities, Asbury or the world. The need is obvious, so it has to begin somewhere. Could it begin at Asbury, something that would really shake our world for God?' In the early church, with individuals, there was a deep hunger for God. Where does it begin? It begins in our own lives because we are hungry for God himself. I realized that God was working in my own life. There was within me a holy awareness and a deep moving of God's spirit. At times, it seemed like a life and death struggle. Not an hour passed that I did not feel the Holy Spirit interceding, and even in my sleep, I found my soul crying out to God.

"Personally, I cannot pray nor have the strength to intercede. The only way it's possible is through the Holy Spirit through me. I underscore this that the Holy Spirit is interceding in a measure quite unknown to me to powerfully move. It is not me. It is God. When or how God will move, I don't know. He told me to be steady; He wanted me to pray and wait for Him."

Chapter Twenty-Eight

JEANNINE....WHEN JESUS WALKED IN AND REVIVAL CAME

"It was a difficult time on campus. I had students come to me before the end of the year and they would say, 'Jeannine, you pray, we know that you care. The high school students are getting their drugs from the college students. We need God to come on this campus.' I went to Dr. (Dennis) Kinlaw and told him what I had heard. I said, 'Dr. Kinlaw, don't worry, God is going to come.'

"Well, how did I know this? In a fast and prayer meeting, this altar was filled. I couldn't believe it. It was an all-time spiritual low on campus and I said to one of the students, I wish we could pray all night. We had curfew at 10 o'clock. So, once again, a very shy student went to see Dean Spann. I said, I want to ask you a very unusual request. God is working in the men's dorm and the women's dorm. We men and women students would like to get together and intercede all night if possible. Would that be possible? Well, he was silent. Totally silent. He said, 'I'll do it under two conditions. You take full responsibility for any women students who sign out, and we'll make only one announcement. No publicity.'

"So when the announcement was made, it was to only a small group of people. So that October 3rd, I came into Hughes. New gold carpet had just been installed. I went back to the sky lights and I said, God, I don't know anything about prayer. I ask You just to come. How, I don't know, but I want You to come. Don't you know, at about 12 a.m., ten men students knelt here at the altar. In 20 minutes, we had 150 students meeting to pray in this auditorium.

"We began to intercede and the Shekinah Glory came. It was a foretaste of the revival that was to come in February. We began to quote Scriptures about Salvation. One quoted II Chronicles 7:14…'If my people who are called by my name will humble themselves, and pray and seek my face, and turn from their wicked ways, then I will hear from Heaven, and will forgive their sin, and will heal their land.' Lord, we have sinned against You. We want You to come. We began to sing, and we literally lifted the rafters. I'd never seen anything like this in my life. I went up into the balcony, watching it all in total awe. God had come. And there was only one professor present, and he found me up there, dear brother C.V. Hunter. He said to me, 'Jeannine, I'm trying to figure out who's in charge here?' I said, Dr. Hunter, I believe it is the Holy Spirit. He said, 'Don't you think that He's met us?'

"There were 80 of us students still in the auditorium at 3 a.m. in the morning. We formed a chain all around the altar and back up here in front of the pulpit. We thanked God that He was going to come. The next morning, we had chapel at 8 o'clock. I got to bed at 4 a.m. and was back here at 8 o'clock for chapel. Well, chapel came and went and nothing happened. I came down here and a student caught me and said, 'Jeannine, nothing happened and I said, do you know Acts 1:7…'It's not for you to know times or the seasons which the Father has put in my hands. But you shall receive power.' He's coming.

"In a desire to have God work in a deeper way, we adapted the John Wesley Great Experience and we presented it to the leadership of the student body to get involved that October. Six students committed for 30 days to pray 30 minutes, get into the Word, journal what God was saying to them and share their faith each day. We would meet once each week to check up on each other. At the beginning of the winter term in January, 1970, 30 student leaders did the John Wesley Great Experiment. We presented our testimonies as an option for students to get involved in a small group on that day. Slips of paper began to come in for students to be in a small group and this was Monday, February 2.

"On February 3, I went downstairs to pray. I came up and sat back there in the junior section. My chapel partner said to me, 'I have a test the next hour.' I said, I do, too. She said, 'But I don't feel that I am going to take it. Do you feel that way, too?' I said, "Yes, I feel that way too." She said, 'But how is it going to happen?' The person we saw that was going to speak, we didn't know how God was going to do this through him. Well, God had everything in control. He had the academic dean in charge.

"So he stood up and he said, 'I'm not going to speak. I'm opening it for testimonies. So over across the auditorium from me, Larry Sutherland, the Gym Jamboree clown, stood up and said, 'I've been a hypocrite but God has got a hold of my life.' He started sharing and another started sharing and pretty soon you couldn't hear people, so they had to come up here. There was a line and the altar began to fill. The bell rang for class and my other chapel partner said, 'Jeannine, they can't stop this.' I said, 'You get up there and tell the dean.' So, he approached the dean, as did the same brother, Dr. Hunter, who had been in our prayer meeting that night. So, he spoke with the academic Dean Reynolds. He was the only one that could call off class, and he called off class.

"I went flying out the back at 12 o'clock noon across the street to see a couple of seminary students that I knew. I said, "It's here! It's here!" And they said, "What's here?" I said "It's revival. It's here." I'd already witnessed it the night of prayer on October 3. "Revival is here." They came and no sooner had they walked into the Hughes foyer, tears started running down their cheeks. They sensed the presence of God. It was so obvious.

"That week, I maybe slept 20 hours. I don't remember eating. But when you are in the presence of God, there is nothing more glorious than to see God come in His power and fullness. On February 6, I wrote a friend around 2 a.m. and I felt led to pray out my feelings. I asked God to break me and make me more like Jesus. God was moving so deeply in our midst. I knew this was the outpouring of the Holy Spirit on our campus. It was the answer to the deep longing of my heart for world revival. I knew that this was just the beginning. I, too, needed a fresh touch. I knew that there was always room for spiritual growth in my own life for a closer, more intimate walk with God.

"Revival touches the masses, but it spreads individually, only if we recognize our own shortcomings and check out our own obedience to God. I was never the same after the revival. After my senior year, almost 18 months later, I went to the mission field in Colombia. I was in Spain when Jack Taylor came and spoke. Before he came, I was saying, Lord, I know about revival, but what do you want me to do here? When he spoke, it really touched my heart and I wrote this. 'The coal in my soul burst into flame. Once having lived through the days of the Holy Spirit's obvious deep working, I've never been satisfied with the norm. Regardless of where I am, there is a constant cry in my soul for the reviving of God's people and the awakening of the lost to have a hunger for God. I know it is possible to believe God for the Holy Spirit to send transforming power in His people. I have seen it.

"On the day of the service in Spain, I dashed home for a short siesta. I woke up from a dream that I thought was strange. I tried to shove it off. In my dream, I was ushered into a room where a newborn baby lay. The baby was placed in my arms and an incredible thrill pierced my heart hearing his cry. I was puzzled. Why should I be holding this new life first? The baby wasn't mine. Why should I be so privileged? While trying to grasp this, the Lord began to speak to me.

"Lord, what are you trying to say? The baby. That's the revival I have seen. As I hurried to catch the subway to the service, the Holy

Spirit spoke to me, 'Jeannine, all that you have seen and witnessed up to now is the birth of a great revival. You know the wonder of a new born baby and it's a wonder to everybody. It's the center of attention. Then the baby grows and develops and others tend to not notice as much. But the ones caring for the little one are aware of the signs of growth. Prayer has this role in revival.'

"'The revival of 1970 did not die. Today, my Spirit continues to bring new light. You have beheld revival in infancy. Believe now for full maturity. If you believe, you will see the glory of God. Humanly, it is impossible to capture in a few words the glimpse I saw as God pulled back the curtains of eternity. An awesome awareness flooded my soul.

"In conclusion about the 1970 revival, in Hebrew thought, the 50th year is the year of the Jubilee. What does the year of Jubilee mean? Jubilee is the restoration of what has been lost. So, 2020 is the year that God is coming. He's here."

Jeannine's message followed with a rousing response from the audience, many of whom witnessed the 1970 revival with her and were overjoyed to hear her tell her story. It was more than one could express, the joy of being in an audience of people who had witnessed one of the greatest movements of God in the history of America. Everyone who was at Asbury during the revival, and were at this service, rejoiced in reliving the mighty presence of God in Hughes Auditorium once again. For them, the memory never fades. Coming together again and recalling those days as college students, and hearing Jeannine share her heart was an unbelievable, Glory Hallelujah time of rejoicing. It just lit a hunger to see it happen, not only again at Asbury, but across America and throughout the world.

Chapter Twenty-Nine
TIM PHILPOT SKIPS CHAPEL BUT FINDS THE REVIVAL

This two-hour chapel service had one more speaker, retired Judge Tim Philpot, a 1973 Asbury graduate, who was gloriously saved during the 1970 revival as a freshman. His revival and conversion story as a student has already been told in chapter eleven of this book, but he added more interesting things about his early life and how God has used him as a strong and powerful witness across America and 67 countries. It all resulted by the inspiration of a changed life from the revival.

He began by saying, "Although Jeannine and I had not spoken about what we were going to say, she had no idea that I was going to open with Leviticus 25, which is about the Year of Jubilee. Verse 10 says, "Set this year apart as holy…2020. A time to proclaim freedom throughout the land to all who live there." And then, he read verses 54 and 55 and said he wanted to substitute Asbury for Israel. "If any Asburians have not been brought back by the time the Year of Jubilee arrives, they and their children must be set free at that time. For the people of Asbury belong to me. They are my servants whom I brought out of the land of Egypt. I am the Lord your God."

Tim told about his parents and his unlikely early beginnings that turned his family toward the great Christian institution of Asbury. "My story is about a little boy named Timmy. It's actually found in Galatians 1:15-16. 'Even before I was born, God chose me and called me by his marvelous grace.' My parents married in 1940 at Renfro Valley here in Kentucky. My father was a hillbilly drunk. My mother was a person who would end up making all A's at Asbury College someday. They didn't really fit each other. My Dad got drunk and signed up for the Marines. I have the letters he wrote from Parris Island in 1942 to my mother. They are like reading letters from Barney Fife.

"My parents were separated for three and a half years. When my Dad returned home from the war in 1945, his alcoholism got worse, and in 1947, he was in a sanitarium. My mother, who had been saved in a little Methodist church in Newtown, Ohio under an Asbury student pastor named Don Porteus, began to pray for her husband. He and my mother concocted a scheme to get my Dad enrolled in Asbury College in 1947. Dr. C.T. Johnson was the president. Don talked Dr. Johnson into letting my father enroll even though he had not graduated from high school.

"My mother was a skilled secretary, and she got a job here working in the business office. My parents enrolled as freshmen in 1947, the same time as the fall revival in 1947. My Dad, who was still slipping off to Lexington to drink on the weekends, got hooked into a prayer meeting here someplace with some of his friends including Tom Ditto. It was a miracle that my Dad was saved that night and he started preaching the next Sunday morning. By February of 1950, he was part of a revival on this campus in this auditorium.

"I never heard much of the details about the February, 1950 revival, but I would suspect that one of the things my parents prayed for at that time was children. They had been told they would never have any children. So, they graduated from here in June, 1950, and in March of 1951, a little boy named Timmy was born. And then came Danny, who is here this morning. The word I kept hearing during my childhood was that Timmy and Danny are miracles. God must have a plan for them.

"The plan wasn't going so well. By the time I was 14, I was such a rotten little kid, and my parents shipped me off to a boarding school in Florida, which is where I met Jeannine Brabon for the first time. But then I believe, and I think it is true for everyone in this room, God chose me and called me by his marvelous grace. And then, the verse says, 'It pleased him to reveal his Son to me.' That's the 1970 for me.

"On January 11, 1970, it was Super Bowl Sunday, 50 years ago and the Kansas City Chiefs won, just as they did yesterday. I had a little gold Mustang convertible and was driving way too fast. I had a young lady in the car with me, and we were trying to get to Lexington to watch the Super Bowl. I hit a slick spot and went down a 30-foot embankment with no seat belts, and for about five seconds I was completely sure that I was dead. My precious possession, my Mustang was totaled. Somehow, I survived the accident and so did the young lady.

"Twenty-three days later was February 3, 1970. God got my attention. He will get your attention. He'll take away your Mustang. He'll let you see what death looks like. So on February 3, I was skipping chapel. I was actually studying up for an Old Testament exam. I was one of those students who was pretty sure that the Rapture had come when I went to the classroom and no one was there. I wandered over here and pretended like I was happy with everything.

"By February 6, at 1 a.m. on Friday morning, I stood at the back of the auditorium and I grabbed a young lady who was next to me. I have even forgotten who she was. You saw on the video this morning that I told her that I didn't think I was a Christian. She said, 'I know. But there are five guys downstairs praying for you right now.' I came running down to the altar right there (pointing to the place). Lots of people surrounded me who were praying for me, including Steve Seamands. I met a gentleman that's here today who said he was one of those people, and I haven't seen him in 50 years.

"So, it was good that He revealed His Son not just for me, but so that I would proclaim the Good News about Jesus to the Gentiles. It started first with my brother Danny when I went to his school in Lexington at Tates Creek High School. My brother, some of my old golf brothers and others, got saved when revival broke out. The next week, I was off to Minneapolis at a Bible college and revival broke out there. I put a little sign on my golf bag, 'Christ died for my sins.' I started wearing this fish hook which I have on today. People would ask, what is the fish hook? I would just say, Jesus said, follow me and I will make you fishers of men. I have been doing that for 50 years and I have a sack of them with me if you want one.

"So, God said for me to proclaim the Gospel to the Gentiles and for me, the Gentiles have been mostly lawyers, judges and politicians and golfers. I have preached in 67 countries, but most of my best work has been eyeball to eyeball with lawyers and heathens, sharing the Good News of Jesus. I close with this, something I got from Dr. Robert Coleman, one of the heroes of the revival. It is Revelation 12:11…'They overcame him by the blood of the lamb, by the word of their testimony and they were not afraid to die.' I feel that we should have an invitation today, but it's not one to success and glory. It is an invitation to suffer and for trouble that comes into our lives.

"John in Revelation 1:9 was exiled to Patmos for two things…for preaching the Word of God and for his testimony about Jesus. Revelation 6:9, the souls that were martyred for the Word of God and for being faithful in their testimony. Revelation 24…Souls that were beheaded for their testimony about Jesus and for proclaiming the Word of God. You will only get in trouble for the rest of your life for two things, the Word of God, if you believe it, and your testimony for Jesus.

"Fifty years later, I can give you testimony that He has been faithful to me, that the Word of God has meant everything to me. What happened to me here was profound in my life, but the most life changing experience came ten years later. I began to get out of the bed early every morning to what I called a Dew Ranch Life, when the dew is still on the grass. I would spend an hour or two in the Word of God, eating the Word of God, and then my testimony became real to me and the people around me. My prayer for you today is, are you eating the Word of God? Do you have a testimony of Jesus, not of Asbury or your goodness, but a testimony of what Jesus has done in your life? What a day this would be, the year of the Jubilee.

"Lord Jesus, would you set this year, 2020, apart as holy? Would you make this a time to proclaim freedom throughout the land for all who live here? Lord Jesus, if there is anybody here today who has not experienced the freedom that is found in Jesus Christ, I pray that they would claim that same freedom that I received 50 years ago. If any Asburians have not been brought back over these last 50 years, I pray that they and their children would be set free at this time. For the people of Asbury belong to you; they are your servants and You are their Lord and their God. Lord Jesus, if there is any person here today, any student, any visitor here who has not received that freedom that is in Jesus Christ, I pray that You would give them courage as we close to come to this altar and find that freedom that is found in Jesus Christ. Amen

Tim Philpot at the reunion

Chapter Thirty

THE 50TH REVIVAL REUNION ENDED WITH AN ALTAR CALL, TESTIMONIES, AND A HYMN SING OF PRAISE

After such a testimony by an Asbury freshman in 1970, who went on to give his life in service to God as an attorney and judge in Lexington, Kentucky, it was only right to end this special chapel service with an invitation, an altar call for salvation, confession, repentance and more re-commitment and re-dedication to the Lord Jesus.

Chaplain Haseloff, in giving the invitation said, "Thousands have met with the Lord in this room. Thousands have knelt at this altar and have confessed sin. They have had burdens lifted. They have received callings and have been filled with the Holy Spirit. Much has been surrendered here and many people have stood at this altar with the assurance that they belong to Jesus. And so, as we respond to Him this morning, we come also to Him to intercede, to petition God, to bring renewal in our hearts, to bring revival to our churches, to bring awakening to our land.

"So, as the praise band leads us in song, you are invited to this altar. You are invited to make your seat an altar if you chose to find fulfillment in the promise that those who seek Him will find Him." So, as the praise band began with instrumental music, they began to sing *How Great Is Our God*. Slowly, many Asbury students from the 1970 revival began to make their way once again to the altar and other guests who had come to this revival celebration. Students left their seats and came forward to kneel and pray.

The praise band moved into *Great Are You Lord*, as the presence of the Lord was so real and divine. You couldn't help but think that this is a little taste of 1970 and other movements of God in this place. Then, the band sang softly *How Great Thou Art*, as many in the audience would sing along, feeling the Spirit penetrate deep into their hearts. The invitation lasted for 30 minutes, and by now, it was 12:30 and time for a special lunch for the 1970 students and their guests.

They slowly made their way to the Johnson Hall Cafeteria in the middle of the campus and served their trays from the many selections of food, quite different from lunch times in 1970. What a joy it was for those in their 70's to feel like a college student again. Some 250 took seats in rows of tables in the Gray Room. After a few minutes, Lisa Harper of the Asbury Alumni Office gave students the opportunity to give a memory of the 1970 revival. One by one, the former students stood, when a microphone was handed to them, and gave more touching stories and testimonies with such passion and delight; all anxious to tell their story. That time had to be brought to an end at almost 2:30. Everyone has a story, and you wanted to hear them all. It was simply glorious and thrilling to hear such remembrances.

Jeannine speaking at the alumni luncheon

The Asbury leaders wanted guests to have time to visit the Revival display in the Kinlaw Library and the Eagle Outlet in the Hamann-Ray Building. Hughes Auditorium was open for prayer. At 3:30, there was a Coffee Break in the upper level of Kinlaw Library, and at 4 p.m., author Rebecca Price Janney would render a reading from her newly published fiction book, *Sweet, Sweet Spirit*, about the 1970 Asbury Revival. That took place in the Kinlaw Library Board Room hosted by the English Department.

The 1970 Revival Celebration concluded at 7 p.m. in Hughes Auditorium with a Revival Hymn Sing led by Danny Key, class of 1973. Danny is Director of the Seminary Singers at the Asbury Theological Seminary. He was chosen by Lisa Harper to have such an honor of leading in this glorious service of song and praise. Hymn Sings at Asbury are highly cherished occasions, in which alums and friends of Asbury will drive hundreds of miles to participate and experience. It was only appropriate to end the 50th revival anniversary with a Hymn Sing of praise.

Danny began by saying that he was in the 1970 chapel service as a freshman, and Larry Sutherland, the first student to stand and give testimony that morning, was his hall monitor in the men's dormitory. He had seen a dramatic change in Larry's life.

Danny explained that shortly before the 50th Reunion, he had rediscovered an album that Professor Jack Rains had produced a year after the revival. He was head of the Music Department at Asbury. The album featured a reunion medley of songs arranged by Dr. Rains, class of 1941. So, Danny decided to start the Hymn Sing with the same pattern of songs on the album. It also included a beautifully written prose about the 1970 revival. It is believed to be written by Dorothy Best Rains, wife of Dr. Rains. She was a professor of speech at Asbury and a wonderful writer. Dick McClain would narrate the prose in between revival hymns. Dick was an Asbury graduate and affiliated with TMS Global Mission. Danny also had his niece, Kaylyn Moran, Class of 2010, to be the soloist, and Kerry Dorrell and Johnny Dean were pianists for the singing of the hymns.

The audience was thrilled as Lynn Smith, who played the piano for most songs sung during the 1970 revival, played the prelude consisting of the revival hymns. She is also Stu Smith's mother and what a joy it was to hear her piano artistry 50 years later. Danny had the audience to begin with the chorus of *To God Be The Glory*. Then Dick McClain began the revival narration.

And the Spirit of God moved in the hearts of His people at Asbury College. This was a deep unsettling movement, which caused many children of God to seek His face anew, who asked and did wait for Revival. Very early in the morning, God blanketed the earth with snow, then sent the sun to glisten on the whiteness. Our feet crunched on the snow as we crowded into Chapel and then, a hush.

At 10 o'clock on February third, God's Spirit became a palpable presence in Hughes Memorial Auditorium. A student said in his heart, I will always remember this day.

How wonderful for God will give us just one day to be filled with His presence and love to treasure through all our lives. That student was mortal. He saw through a glass darkly for that day was just the beginning of many days, and weeks and months of God's Spirit moving among us.

He moved some to give verbal witness of what God was doing in their hearts. He moved others to prostrate themselves at the altar of prayer. He moved some to seek the company of fellow believers they had sinned against, confessions, forgiveness, embracing, rejoicing. We watched in wonder as God worked. We could not eat. We could not sleep. We had no need of food or rest. For through those hours came heavenly showers. God sent His Spirit as our guest.

Then, Professor Key's next hymn was the revival standard, *There's a Sweet, Sweet Spirit In This Place* followed by this narration.

And as we sat and sang, or knelt and prayed, or stood and spoke, our hearts were melted. Our souls were stirred by God's touch even as the woman who pressed through the throne to touch the hem of his garment, so were many this day made whole and well by his touch. As one wrote, I felt his touch so full of love upon my heart, upon my brow. Jesus, I'm coming now.

Next came the song, *He Touched Me* with another narration.

In introspection, now I see an end to selfishness and strife. I cannot fathom all things, God now possesses all my life. What happened here, I'll never forget or even can I be the same, nor do I comprehend it yet. But this I know, His Spirit came. I bow in adoration, praise to One who gave His life for me. Revived, renewed, refreshed my days. His grace is mine. How can it be.

Then Danny had the joyful singers stand and sing two powerful songs of the Cross, *And Can It Be* and *When I Survey The Wondrous Cross*. It's different when you hear people sing who had committed their all to Jesus. Then Dick McClain gave the final moving narration.

Yes, God's wonderful Spirit invaded us on that February third. He came to cleanse, purify and to empower. So great was His power that it could not be contained here in Hughes Auditorium. It spread out to the community, to Lexington, to other colleges, to universities, to seminaries and to churches. It spread to nearby states, then states further away. The fire spread to Canada, to Honduras, to Columbia. Wherever witness of God's revival goes, special anointing accompanies the witness. Sinners are converted, faltering Christians are restored, believers are sanctified and the end is not yet. In the summer, Asbury students and faculty members gave witness in 50 states and on five continents to what was begun in our midst. And there were also many other things, which Jesus did through the revival. Were every one of these to be written, I suppose the world itself could not contain the books that would be written. To our great God be all the Glory.

After such a breathtaking narration of God's mighty movement here in Hughes Auditorium 50 years prior, the Hymn Sing continued with these powerful hymns of the faith. They were: *To God Be the Glory; O For a Thousand Tongues to Sing; A Mighty Fortress is Our God; Wonderful Grace of Jesus; Blessed Assurance; All Hail the Power of Jesus Name; Great is Thy Faithfulness*; and *It is Well With My Soul.*

Then as with any Asbury event, it ended with an extended time of prayer. Dick McClain read Jeremiah 29:11 and emphasized verses 12 and 13…"Then you will call upon Me and go and pray to Me, and I will listen to you. And you will seek Me and find Me, when you search for Me with all your heart." He asked that it be a prayer of gratitude for all He has done. He asked for God to stir up a deeper hunger in our hearts for more and more of Him.

Then he quoted Psalms 85:6…"Will You not revive us again, That Your people may rejoice in You." The prayer time ended with a request for God to do a fresh work in us, renew our Spirit and never cease to pray for revival, knowing that whatever we can think or imagine it to be, that it would be way too small.

After the singing of the Doxology, the grand and glorious celebration of the 1970 Asbury revival had ended, only to see those students of revival head back to their places of service, seeking for a worldwide revival and awakening that they know is sure to come. *"Praise God from whom all blessings flow. Praise Him all creatures here below. Praise Him above ye heavenly hosts. Praise Father, Son and Holy Ghost. Amen."*

Chapter Thirty-One
CALL TO REVIVAL

"*Restore us, O God; Cause Your face to shine, and we shall be saved*"…Psalm 80:3

A Call to Revival is the only appropriate way to end this historic revival story.

America is ripe for revival. People hunger for revival. The world's greatest need is Jesus. The Bible contains the answer for a nation and world that is filled with sin, corruption, idol worship, immorality, wickedness, evil and ungodliness as in the days of Noah, and Sodom and Gomorrah. We have lost our fear of God. Masses have ignored God. What lies ahead is either revival or judgment, or, perhaps both.

Christians are praying as never before for revival and for another great awakening that will be the greatest our nation has ever witnessed. We are destined for revival and a great awakening. There is a difference in the two, and *Ireland's Lost Heritage* defines the two. "A revival could be described as 'a visitation of God's Spirit on God's people,' but 'an Awakening' as 'a time of such intense visitation that both Christian and non-Christian communities are affected…Revivals alter the lives of individuals, Awakenings alter the world view of a whole people or culture.'"

More prayer groups have emerged across America over the past ten years than any time in our history. People are earnestly praying for revival and another great awakening. Prayer movements, prayer rallies in stadiums, prayer gatherings even on the internet and social media, and an increased prayer emphasis in churches are all desperately sending out a heart cry for revival. Multitudes of prayer warriors are praying. Something remarkable is happening. A sense of expectancy is in the air. Some believe that revival has already started. It must start with personal revival.

Over the past five years, we have seen pockets and movements of revival that are a foretaste of what is to come. The only thing that will save America is an awakening that will impact believers and unbelievers from coast to coast. A mighty movement of God in America would also spread throughout the world. It will require that all Christians take prayer seriously.

The students at Asbury College had one simple prayer. It was that Jesus would come to their campus. As they prayed, they believed and expected Him to come. They would say, "Do you think Jesus will come today? Do you think He will come tomorrow?" They believed and expected Him to come, and in chapel one winter morning, He did. We must pray as if revival and the next great awakening depends upon our own personal praying. We must believe that prayer is the only thing that can save America. We must consider ourselves revivalist watchmen who alert the people that revival is coming, and this includes every person who is reading these pages and knows that revival is our only hope.

We have this precious promise from Almighty God in II Chronicles 7:14…"If my people who are called by my name, will humble themselves and pray and seek My face and turn from their wicked ways, then I will hear from Heaven, and forgive their sin and heal their land." God has given us this promise, and he will keep it if every Christian in American is in earnest prayer. If they are, Revival

CALL TO REVIVAL • 137

and Awakening would come to America. We must care enough. We must agonize and plead for Jesus to come in His Glory. Otherwise, America will drift further and further away from God.

Revival never comes the same way twice. We've seen revivals and awakenings begin with individuals such as Jeremiah Lanphier, a 48-year-old layman in the Reformed Dutch Church in New York City, in 1857. He posted signs for a noon prayer meeting. Six people showed. Twenty came the next week, and then 30 to pray at a time when church attendance was rapidly declining. The stock market crashed and noon prayer by businessmen spread across America. In two years, one million people came to Christ out of a population of 30 million people. The 1857-59 Laymen's Revival impacted the entire nation.

It can and must happen again. Sin is rampant. Millions of lives are at stake for their eternal destiny. People are dying and going to Hell every day. They are blinded to the Truth. Deception is rampant. Jesus must come in Shekinah Glory, which our nation and world have missed and desperately need. Revival comes to usher in the divine presence of God.

The next movement of God could come through a child, a teenager, a college student, or someone like 26-year-old Evan Roberts, a coal miner, who passionately prayed in the Wales Revival in 1904. It could start with praying women, businessmen or even a worn-out preacher. It could start in a country church or a mega church. The 1949 Hebrides Revival near Scotland began with Peggy and Christine Smith, two praying ladies in their 80s. One was blind. William J. Seymour, a 35-year-old, one-eyed African American preacher started The Azusa Revival in Los Angeles, which lasted from 1906-1915.

Perhaps another movement of God would start again on a college campus, which would spark revival on every college campus in America. College students on fire for God can ignite revival across America and the world with their boundless energy and passion for God. This happened at Asbury, a small college hidden away in

Kentucky, when coed Jeannine Brabon started praying. Wherever the place or whomever God choses, should we not be revivalist watchmen, telling people that revival is coming?

In the Book of Ezekiel, chapter 37, God heard Ezekiel's cry to revive a nation that had grown cold, was hard of heart, was going through the motions of ministry, and was spiritually dead. God heard Ezekiel's prayer and the dry bones were shaken, the winds of the Spirit blew on them, they stood on their feet, and a great army of God stood up from a dead nation to live, fight and die for God Almighty. He is waiting to do it again, this time in America. This will inspire nations throughout the world for revival.

Fervent prayer of Christians in America will bring Shekinah Glory that will shake and shift America back to being a Christian nation again. As a watchman for God, Ezekiel warned the nation Israel that one day God will have His way with us. He warned that 'enough is enough.' Fifty-nine times in Ezekiel, we find these words, "Then, you shall know that I am the Lord." Judgment day is coming soon in America if Americans do not repent. He will come in judgment and show forth His power and supreme reign where every knee shall bow and every tongue shall confess that Jesus Christ is Lord.

God has promised to shake Heaven and earth for revival..."whose voice then shook the earth; but now He has promised, saying, Yet once more I shake not only the earth, but also Heaven"...Hebrews 12:26. Revival is a direct result of God's mercy. Billy Graham said, "There is only one person that can bring revival, and that is the Holy Spirit." He said it in 1949 and again in 2012, "And we're praying for an old-fashioned, Heaven sent, Holy Ghost revival that will sweep our nation from coast to coast." God will shake Heaven and earth, and will come, if we are willing to pay the price in passionate prayer and fasting.

Asbury College President Dr. Dennis Kinlaw was asked, "To what do you attribute this revival?" He responded, "It was as if Jesus walked in and He never left." That's what happened at Asbury. All

1,100 students were impacted by the presence of Jesus in those seven days. Students and faculty lost all sense of time. Food and sleep were not important. Money, either. Classes were dismissed and all anyone could talk about was the revival that was taking place on their campus. For those students, the fire of revival has remained in them for 50 years. They witnessed the Glory like few have.

When revival comes like that in America, what will it be like? Sports and entertainment, the quest for materialism and affluence, and the hunger for power and control will fade. The joy of knowing Jesus will dominate conversation above all other interests. Political leaders will unify and seek God for guidance to govern in ways best for the people. The media will report the news in an unbiased manner… balanced, responsible and accountable. Intellectuals, liberal university professors, atheists and skeptics will humble themselves as little children, and discover and embrace the love of Jesus.

True revival will restore Bible reading and prayer in our public schools. Abortion, at last, will no longer be our great and shameful national sin and will be abolished. Crime will diminish to a low degree. Drug lords and gangs in cities will see their leaders come to know Christ as Savior. We will be amazed to see infamous people delivered from sinful and godless agendas to become radiant Christians. Church attendance will reach an all-time high. Millions of people, not thousands, will cry out to Jesus for salvation and profess faith in Him to save their souls.

Revivals come unexpectedly and are never in a hurry, but when the fire falls from Heaven, it is like a mighty rushing wind. It moves swiftly and spreads rapidly. John Kilpatrick, former senior pastor of the Brownsville Assembly of God Church in Pensacola, Florida, said that his church had intense prayer for revival for two and a half years. On Father's Day in 1995, John says, "I got up that day. I was depressed and didn't want to go to church. We had been praying for revival, but before the sun went down in the west about 6 or 7 o'clock in the evening, I was a different man. My life had completely changed. My future and my destiny had completely changed in less than 12 hours. It could happen to you, too." Jesus walked in that day and the revival became known worldwide. Over the next five years, four million people came from around the globe to their church, and nearly 200,000 people were saved.

May Pentecost fall on America as it did there. May we see Habakkuk 2:14 be manifested in a great awakening movement of God which states, "For the earth will be filled with the knowledge of the glory of the Lord, as the waters cover the sea." As it says in Isaiah 9:7, "The zeal of the Lord will accomplish (or perform) this." If the Everlasting Father can create the heavens and the earth in six days, his boundless power can shake America with revival never seen or heard before. We must pray, believe and expect His divine visitation and intervention. The time has come and time is short. "Look up, for your redemption draws near," Luke 21:28.

We must not forget that the central thrust of revival is to bring us back to the Cross. Without the Good News of the Gospel of Jesus, where on the Cross He conquered death, hell and the grave, we could not have an awakening to save the lost from the misery of their sins, and from a depressed life and shame. The Gospel gives the unsaved a clean slate. They experience a brand new life of love, joy and peace, and escape from a life of misery to a life of purpose and jubilation in Jesus Christ. God grant us a passion for souls so that no one goes to Hell unloved, unwarned or unprayed for.

Leonard Ravenhill, the powerful revival preacher and man of prayer, said, "Next year is not ours. Tomorrow may be too late. Unless we repent now, unless we return and fire the prayer altars now, unless we fast and weep now, woe unto us at the judgment."

O God, thank you for revival praying Christians and prayer warriors who are desperate to see revival. More so, we hunger for a Great Awakening with an energy at which our nation and world shall tremble in revival power, before Your soon return to this earth. Will you pray without ceasing for fire from Heaven to descend? Will you give us the greatest touch of God that America and this world have ever seen? We believe there is a deeper work of God that awaits us. May we earnestly and passionately pray, believing and expecting you to come in Shekinah Glory. May we see waves of your majesty, Glory, and amazing love cover this nation and earth just as waters cover the seas. May Jesus Christ be praised. And we give you all the praise, glory and honor because only You can send revival. May it come quickly, Lord Jesus. Amen.

ABOUT THE AUTHOR

Wayne Atcheson is presently the historian and regional director of the Billy Graham Library in Charlotte, North Carolina where he became its first director in 2006. *The Asbury Revival* is Wayne's eighth book. A student of Bible Prophecy and Revival History, he has also written accounts of recent revival movements in the Southeast.

Prior to his role at the Billy Graham Library, Wayne served with the Jerry B. Jenkins Christian Writers Guild in Colorado Springs, Colorado with the purpose of raising up a new harvest of Christian writers. From 1983-2002, he was Sports Information Director and Associate Director of TIDE PRIDE, the football donor program, at the University of Alabama.

Wayne has a long history with the Fellowship of Christian Athletes. He served on the national FCA staff in Kansas City and Indianapolis from 1967-1979, and was advisor of the Alabama FCA chapter for 18 years. He authored *Impact For Christ*, the 40-year history of the national FCA in 1994, and was major contributor to *Sharing The Victory*, the 50-year history. Other works have been of Alabama Christian athletes and coaches and other Christian biographies.

A native of Chilton County, Alabama, growing up in Maplesville and Clanton, Wayne holds journalism degrees from Samford

University and the University of Alabama. He and his wife, Barbara, have been married for 48 years and their two daughters Elizabeth (Jared) Poplin and Amy Snyder have given them four grandsons, Jack, Luke, Giles and Christian.